THE AMERICAN IDEA OF

Freedom

How Liberty Depends on Property Rights & General Education

GARY J. QUINN

ISBN: 1482661055

ISBN 13: 9781482661057

Library of Congress Control Number: 2013904607

CreateSpace Independent Publishing Platform

North Charleston, South Carolina

TO
THE CITIZENS
OF
THE UNITED STATES

CONTENTS

PROLOGUE

Why American History Is Important

During the Cold War a Russian communist was asked whether he was willing to admit that the American form of democracy was a success. He said, "I don't know. It is too early to tell. It is only 200 years old."

This Russian probably did not think much of American democracy, but rather than condemning it outright he had the good sense not to jump to conclusions. His answer recognized the difficulty of foreseeing the long-range outcomes of wide-scale social-political restructuring. One reason this is interesting is that Marxism in Russia was an attempt to forget the past and try something new. Traditional institutions and customs had to be dismantled to clear the deck for an advanced social order. But here was one communist who was not quick to ignore history and the lessons it can teach. He seemed to be aware that major social and political changes have unforeseen implications that take time to recognize. America's struggle for independence was too new to assess, he thought, but history would eventually judge its worth. Possibly he also wondered how history would treat his own country's socialist efforts.

Another reason his response is interesting is that it reveals an important feature of historical knowledge: it can measure change. Change continually happens, but not always in obvious ways. Social and political adjustments may take place gradually and go unnoticed for a long time unless they are seen in relation to the past. Even if this Russian were to admit the value and creativity of our Founders' experiment, he still might not be ready to endorse it because the original insights could be lost over time and the country would no longer be what it once was. Only time would tell.

He was right that sociopolitical changes takes place slowly and are hard to assess at any given time. Still, one would think that 200 years should be long enough to provide some useful lessons. Even shorter periods can be instructive. Had the Soviets paid more attention to their own history they may have recognized the developing faults of the socialist-communist system earlier and corrected them before they became obvious to the whole world and did so much damage in Russia and elsewhere.

Perhaps there is a lesson here for Americans. If the current reformers who want to forget history and transform the country into a totally fair and equitable society would acknowledge the importance of historical perspective, it might help them better recognize errors, identify trends and evaluate prospects. Our democracy may be new on the world scene but it does have a track record. Hopefully it is long enough to give us clues to what is actually happening to our democracy and provide indications about its future.

This book is about our beginnings as a free republic, but it is not just about the past – it is our story too. It tells of the original American idea of freedom, how it has affected the nation and what it means for us in our time. Presenting an understanding of freedom based on the context of American history is important because of the way freedom is understood today. Whereas the traditional meaning of freedom conveyed a definite way of life, "freedom" now has become just a word that can justify almost anything to anyone. This shift in meaning has unsettling implications.

Early on, freedom, independence and liberty had specific meaning to American leaders. They associated these terms with the struggle against England and also with its aftermath. The war with England was only one aspect of the Revolution. The other was the republican form of government that emerged from it. It was widely known that this new government was an experiment. There had been republics in the past but the question was whether or not this one, national in scale and comprising so many different cultural, religious and political elements, could survive for any length of time. Could the people govern themselves through their representatives, or would the experiment only show that kingly, dictatorial authority must inevitably reassert itself? There was great hope, but no assurance of success.

Once the War was won, it became evident that intense efforts were needed to create political and social conditions appropriate for the new Republic. The task of promoting the foundations of American freedom consumed the energies of many Founders for many years. One of the most energetic and articulate among them was Noah Webster. Although not as familiar to us today as other Founders, he was well-known then and important for us now because of his unusual ability to spell out the essential meaning of American freedom. He was able to do this because he was not a newcomer to the idea and practice of this special form of liberty. He belonged to a family that had been in this country for over 150 years and had developed ideas about freedom that he inherited, lived and expressed in ways that were meaningful then, and still are today.

Webster is a good place to start with America's tale of freedom because of his background and commitment, and because of his skills in describing and promoting two fundamentals of American-style freedom – namely, property rights and general education. But his story is not unique. He was one among many who shared this common vision. A look at his and other Founders' thinking on these two subjects helps highlight the differences between their vision and certain current attitudes toward freedom, and brings into sharper focus their inventive approach to fostering it on a national scale.

An outline of some of their contributions follows, but it must be said that an exhaustive study of any of them would require much more than is intended here. The sole purpose of this work is to highlight the importance of private property and general education in early American thinking, and to show relationships to current viewpoints on freedom, some of which ignore, dismiss or distort these fundamentals in part or altogether. This is unfortunate unless we assume, as some have, that the Founders' experiment has failed and should be forgotten as we replace it with stronger government control, or with something else, as yet undefined.

Are These Old White Men Really Dead?

We often hear from advocates of racial and ethnic equality, feminists and other activists that our Founders, far from advancing the cause of freedom, suppressed it by enslaving blacks, oppressing women and killing Indians. Therefore, they say, instead of looking to these hypocritical dead white men for lessons in liberty, we should ignore them and promote a new brand of freedom based on true equality and diversity. This message has found its way into our schools, and in some cases in angry, strident forms. Recently, a school in Oklahoma had a rap-themed program for at-risk students that included a song called "Old Dead White Men." Its lyrics were highly critical of some of our Founders: James Monroe stepped on Indians, women and blacks; Andrew Jackson treated Indians the way Adolph Hitler dealt with Jews. The designers of the program thought such lyrics were appropriate because they caught the students' attention. The problem was that it brought their attention to already negative thoughts about government and authority figures, and misrepresented the history of our early leaders. The good news is that the program was later halted due to objections by teachers, parents and others (Rolland).

This negative attitude, although usually voiced in less crude terms, is not hard to find today. Activists argue that because early American leaders did not promote freedom for all, we should declare these old white men and their so-called principles of freedom dead once and for all. We should stop honoring them, forget their history, except for the damage it has done, and move on to a new, tolerant, inclusive type of free society.

Advocates proposing this want a clean sweep of American traditions, but they are not alone in dismissing the history of this country. Anti-historical views are commonplace.

History Is Bunk – Or Is It?

More than a few ignore or reject American history today. It has become almost beside the point in our schools and is ridiculed by many who insist on what they think are new and creative approaches to political and social matters. Even business leaders have joined in the campaign against history. Consider this statement:

> History is more or less bunk. It's tradition. We don't want tradition. We want to live in the present and the only history that is worth a tinker's dam is the history we made today. (Ford)

This thought by a famous American car-maker blends in nicely with the views of more radical advocates eager to dismantle American traditional ideas and practices. Henry Ford is a useful reference because he was and still is widely admired as an icon of American ingenuity and, as is often the case, is considered an authority in many areas because he was an expert in one area. His status allows critics of history to quote him, not necessarily because they approve of his accomplishments or his overall attitude toward the past, but because he offered pithy statements that illustrate what they want to believe about history.

The use of Ford for anti-historical endorsement is instructive because he was influential and could clearly state his ideas to the "common man." His was not an academic or sophisticated philosophical argument addressed only to the few. Instead, it was an assertion that could be communicated to a very large audience. But he could hardly have literally believed this about history. He was probably overstating his case in order to make a point about not getting bogged down in generalities and useless information. In fact, we know he actually was interested in the kind of history that concerned practical matters and daily life.

However, if we take Ford literally a fallacy immediately becomes apparent. Consider the alternative: What would happen if he actually did ignore history? How would he have known the possibilities of the automobile without awareness of already existing methods of manufacturing carts, wagons, buggies and earlier automobiles? Did he not build on that knowledge to produce his horseless buggies? How would he have discovered all the tools, metals, materials and know-how he used to manufacture cars? They certainly were not all created in the "present." How could he have known, or even thought of, all of them? In fact, they were products of traditional skills. Buggy manufacturing was already a sophisticated, developed industry. If he were to think about it, would he say that all the craftsmen's skills, discoveries and mechanical advances passed along from generation to generation up to his time were "bunk"?

Henry did not need to know who invented the wrench or screwdriver. He probably would assign these facts to his bunk category. But he did have to learn what they were for and how to use them. He probably knew more than a little about tool-making, which is a traditional skill, as well as already existing methods of effective leadership and organization. He applied his own genius to manufacturing and assembly, to be sure, but was building on the ideas that go all the way back to the invention of the wheel. The fact is that Henry's "present" included a huge store of knowledge from the past.

Ignorance: The Tool of Hapless Change

When it comes to the history of American institutions and associated ideas of freedom, those who try to dismiss American political history may do it in the hope that the less known about it, the easier it is to circumvent established ideas and get on to newer, better things. But to understanding the principles and tools of a nation, i.e., the beliefs and institutions it is built upon, knowledge of the past is even more important than the historical knowledge Ford used. That is because national and state institutions are more complex than mechanical tools and manufacturing processes. They are complicated because they are made up of large numbers of human beings with many different goals, and always in a state of flux. A tool or an assembly line can change without altering its primary purpose more easily than a national institution can. It may function successfully for a time, but then become disoriented and ineffective as it loses contact with its founding principles. Being huge organic entities, our local, state and federal institutions are subject to constant change, for good or ill. And because they are not controlled by one or a few men, as Ford Motors once was, political and societal changes are determined by the thinking, goals and behaviors of a great number of people.

It is possible that basic institutions like the Congress or the Judiciary might continue to function as originally intended for a long time, but they also could change so much that they become unrecognizable as Constitutional entities. Since change is inevitable, it seems worthwhile to measure these changes against the founding principles that created them in the first place. If these principles still hold, we would want any changes we make to build upon them. If not, we need to measure them by some other standard or goal to prevent the changes from becoming haphazard and disorienting.

As we pursue new and better things for the present, appreciation of the good things from the past is invaluable. This is certainly true in the case of American political, economic and social life. As historical change takes place, our involvement in it is not isolated from the flow of history that has carried us along to the present. We live in the land of freedom, but freedom can be understood in a number of ways. Should we not acknowledge that the way we think of freedom, even in the most general way, is rooted in our history?

While it may be true that some old notions can be safely forgotten, we should not assume that central American historical ideas are among them. Ignorance of them makes it harder to understand what our political institutions are designed to do, and what the rights and obligations of the citizens are in our Republic. This sort of knowledge is valuable as a starting point even for those who want substantial changes to our political system and way of life. Political systems have a history. They do not appear from nowhere, nor do they change without reference to their past, whether recognized or not.

If we actually did eradicate all references to our beginnings, what should we do with the institutions the Founders left to us? To be consistent, we should ignore them too. We would need to replace or totally revamp the federal legislative, executive and the court systems, the relationship between the states and the federal government and even the Constitution itself. This would of course also erase everyone's current favorite, the First Amendment, now used, rightly or wrongly, to support so many causes. If our old leaders' ideas are dead, we need to create something to replace them. It will not be sufficient to criticize the current status and sing heart-felt songs about freedom. Concrete ideas are required, first of all, defining what this new form of government should be like, and second, how it should be attained. Unexamined references to autonomous freedom, multiculturalism, or socialist theories do not suffice. A clear picture of the intended aim is essential in order to avoid being led by political negativism or a swirl of fuzzy dreams about a utopian future.

This is not to say that reform is unnecessary. It is necessary, as it is in almost every generation, because freedom is not universal. Too many people suffer discrimination, lack of education and undeserved poverty, and remedies must be found. But finding them need not require trashing former leaders who, despite their failings, advanced the cause of freedom to a remarkable degree. In fact, it is from them that we have acquired the political vision of the possibilities of human freedom. Their work has not been completed by any means, but ignoring them could easily result in an unwitting return to the injustices and social pitfalls that they fought against. If that were to happen, the ideas of our Founders might someday once again be "discovered" as something new and exciting.

Over the centuries freedom has meant a variety of things, from almost complete anarchy in weak governments to practically nothing at all in despotic regimes. In Islamic societies, for example, while certain checks and limitations on autocratic tyranny are traditional, freedom in a political sense is unknown. It has meaning only in a personal sense, i.e., one is either a slave or a free person. Their traditions provide for justice, but not for political freedom, as known in America (Lewis). Something similar could be said about medieval Christian Europe. The virtues of justice and charity were embedded in the culture, but not American-style freedom. Serfs may have been treated with decency, but had little say under the rule of kings and nobles. There are examples from all over the world of autocratic rule, sometimes basically just but often crushingly oppressive. Our thinking on political and personal freedom in America is different, and it did not arise from nowhere. It surely must be recognized that our history has had a strong bearing on today's notions and attitudes regarding freedom.

It makes sense to look back in order to see more clearly where we are now, especially as history becomes increasingly irrelevant in our schools and in activist movements that see long-established ideas as obstructions to progress. But it is a natural desire to know and respect the past. Orphans sometimes spend years trying to discover their parents; people study their family genealogies; archaeologists investigate ancient cultures; scientists learn from forerunners in their field. Such investigations uncover more than facts from bygone days; they help people understand the here and now. The Founders of this country were well aware of the advantages of such inquiries. Almost all had biblical training as youths and were influenced by it. Most continued to study it as adults. Some were well-versed in Greek and Roman history, literature and philosophy, as well as later theological-philosophical contributions up to and including the Enlightenment. Knowledge of this kind helped formulate their ideas about the pitfalls and possibilities of peoples and nations. This background and their own life experiences enabled them to form their unique vision of American freedom.

Which Definition of Freedom Do We Want?

Freedom is a subject that everyone talks about, but without much agreement on what it is. Since Americans are known for celebrating and promoting freedom here and around the world, one might think that we possess a general consensus on its meaning. But there are strong reasons to doubt this. For some it may simply mean having money, for others it could mean not working, or having good health. It could mean not being harassed by lawsuits, or getting out of jail or just not being bothered. Freedom could also be seen as something bestowed through government grants, handouts and special privileges. But there are also some who see it simply as knowing the truth, or being able to practice their religion without hindrance, as early Americans did. And there are still many who associate it with self-reliance and communal harmony.

The many conflicting interpretations of freedom that we now have in this country suggest that we have lost or at least have muddled its original American meaning. Fundamentals determine the course of events, as philosophers, theologians, business people, coaches and others have often taught. Vince Lombardi summarized the point by defining football in three words: blocking and tackling. Coaches and players who do not understand and practice those fundamentals are at a huge disadvantage. But fundamentals also apply to social and political matters. Given the present situation, it seems reasonable to take a look at current notions of freedom in American society as they relate to the fundamentals that motivated our Founders.

The many protests these days that support the special interests of feminists, black and white racists, pacifists, union members and political groups may or may not have legitimacy, but whether they do or not, they all seem to justify themselves by appeals to freedom. Each group has an agenda, but the question remains: how can each of these agendas be reconciled with the American idea of freedom for all?

The First Amendment is often cited to legitimize these beliefs and movements. The freedoms of religion, speech, the press and assembly guaranteed there are understood in ways that make personal autonomy, multiculturalism and particular group rights appear to be constitutional. Because aspects of these interpretations are not entirely alien to our history, they influence all Americans to some degree. But people may not realize that early Americans did not think of freedom primarily in these terms. Today the notion of freedom has become much more secular and individualistic than it was at our beginnings.

To ignore the sources of American freedom is to open the door to vague and confusing notions that complicate what was once fairly clear. For one thing, in a free nation we need to know how property rights should be understood. Who decides what these rights are and how they should be exercised? Another thing we need to know is why quality general education is so important in our form of government and who should determine what students are taught in school. Learning our history can help answer these and other questions that puzzle us today. Many problems arise that require more than quick fixes. How do we deal with executive, legislative and judicial branches and agencies that inevitably compete with one another for supremacy and issue conflicting rules? What powers should they have, and how should they be exercised? Why do many citizens believe that moral education is necessary in a democratic society? Why do less than half of the citizens typically vote? These and many other questions are being warmly debated, but unless there are some basic reference points on which to ground the discussion, we just talk past one another.

One of these reference points, and perhaps the most important one, is the concept of American freedom as understood in its historical context. There is a continuum there that provides perspective on how the nation was established and how it has changed, giving insight into how it has retained or strayed from its founding principles. The question today is whether or not it has retained enough of its original spirit to continue as a free republic. If it has, and we want to continue it, renewed efforts are required to support it, but if not, we must spell out as completely as possible what we should look for in the future. Without that, fundamental change could result in anarchy and internal war. If we want to reject the old, what will replace it? Will America become something essentially new, never seen before, or will it return to some form of domination by one or a few rulers under a new name? Will the people at large have a say in it, or will they be subjected to the "wisdom" of autocratic leaders?

It is useful to entertain these questions because today we seem confused about freedom in ways that early Americans were not. We have inherited the fruits of their labors, but the clarity and intensity of their vision has somehow faded. Freedom still means political liberty for the sake of personal liberty, but these days we often think of freedom apart from the grounding principles that motivated our forebears. Unlike them, we may view money, leisure, free speech, not being bothered, or just "winging it" as ends in themselves. And group movements regarding racism, sexism, multiculturalism, militarism and other "-isms" may pursue participants' interests without a sufficient sense, or any sense, of responsibility toward citizens not part of their causes.

Many notions of freedom in use today correlate more or less with each other and with our historical precedents, but others embody views and behaviors that are alien to our history. These recent notions, much more autonomous and secular than before, do not reflect the cultural experience of our people and have seriously challenged it. But before discussing that, we should review some features of that experience.

For much of our history people came here from afar seeking freedom, based on the hope for religious, economic and political independence. The idea of freedom was basically straightforward. People knew what they were seeking and hoped to find it in this new world. Most, although not all, found religious freedom, and most, although not all, found unparalleled economic opportunities, both of which were made possible with the help of a supportive political system.

Freedom Has Never Been Free

An Irishman came to America seeking the freedom and prosperity he had heard about. He had heard the streets were paved with gold. When he got here, however, he discovered the streets were not paved with gold. In fact, they were not paved at all, and it was his job to pave them.

The idea of American freedom has been, and continues to be, a compelling magnet drawing people to our shores. The idea is obvious enough, but its realization has never been guaranteed. The reality is that the road to freedom is not a smooth one. Poor newcomers often discovered this as they struggled to overcome conditions of prejudice and poverty after their arrival. Acceptance and a higher living standard were never attained without cost; they had to be earned.

America has developed economically over the years and more people enjoy a decent standard of living than before. Yet when the people around the world look at us now, they may wonder what American freedom means today. It is especially confusing when they see how we function politically and socially. We should not be surprised by this, since it seems to confuse many of us as well. Freedom means different things to different people. We associate it with democracy and individual liberty, but argue incessantly over the rights and privileges of individuals and groups. We want to know who has these rights and who should have them.

While these disputes are often heated, they still leave the impression that they are matters of interpretation of a generally accepted understanding of American freedom. We know this because each side claims the Constitution is on its side. But the fact is that we do not have an underlying agreement on its meaning. At present what we actually have is a jumble of confusing and conflicting notions of American liberty that are not easily reconciled. Needless to say, this is not a good situation in a country that prides itself on its principles of democratic freedom.

The idea of freedom is a powerful motivator; the way it is understood affects each person's behavior and, in turn, community and national life. This is why the subject, already overworked in a certain sense, needs even more attention than it is getting. The point is not to add more fuel to the fire, but to clarify elements of American freedom that make it unique. A common understanding of freedom would be a unifying force in a country now divided over so many things. This sort of learning starts in the home and is continued in the schools. Higher education offers little at present, and often even adds to the confusion, but it could contribute much. A more informed understanding of American freedom would enhance the general education of all students, and would benefit future teachers, who will influence the next generation. Exposure to the history of the American experiment, if done in an informed, unbiased way, would have a healthy, unifying effect on the whole society.

The Early American Definition of Freedom

If we look back to earlier times, we can see that freedom was not thought of as unrestrained individualism, government giveaways or the celebration of any particular group's special identity. Instead, it was understood in terms of the rights and responsibilities of all citizens as one people. It had to do more with universal justice than with special privileges and separate treatment. Freedom of this kind is a very difficult thing to achieve – so difficult, in fact, that our Constitution stands out as a remarkable blueprint for its promotion. Protests and fevered arguments have always been part of American life, but in the early days people were more concerned with the right to earn and keep freedom than to have it bestowed upon them by government, business or other entities. What they, and especially the Founders, desired most was that people be left free to own and use private property and to have the opportunity to pursue a useful education.

In light of current trends, it may seem strange to us that freedom was grounded in such things. Curtailments of property rights and inattention to general education – especially curriculum and discipline issues – are more accepted now. Expectations of government services have changed. Government then did not exist to furnish a high standard of living or other things we associate with freedom, except to ensure that its pursuit would not be hindered. Beyond national and domestic defense, foreign affairs, inter-state commerce, revenue issues, a court system and a few other things, the government stood aside as citizens made their own way. But it was not just survival of the fittest. The government provided a legal framework for the just treatment of most of the people, although not all. It took time to assimilate some groups, and a war to extend freedom to the slaves.

Early Americans had a vital interest in the right to own land and other forms of property because they served a self-reliant spirit. Individuals were expected to work for their own benefit, but also to cooperate and contribute productively to the community. Given that most of human history is the story of kings and tyrants owning everything, this was an unusual turn of events. Ownership of property was unfamiliar to many early settlers, although they soon recognized its importance. Once here they learned that private property was a possibility, and that achieving it required personal know-how and communal responsibility. This is why our revolutionary leaders had such a strong desire for the education of the many, and not just the elite, as was the practice in Europe. It was seen as a necessary and integral part of the American way of life.

This is not to say that people then did not want to act mainly in their own interest or to identify with their own religious, political or cultural groups. Nor is it to say that they were all superior altruistic beings. Many of their failings are well-known, but what they were striving for and what they actually accomplished is not as well-known today. Although their vision of property rights and quality education has contributed enormously to this nation's prosperity, in recent times it has faded – and with it the early American appreciation of freedom.

PART I
PRIVATE PROPERTY

How Property Rights
Guarantee Freedom

The great and chief end...of men's uniting into commonwealths, and putting themselves under government, is the preservation of their property... (John Locke)

CHAPTER 1

Early American Ideas

I n our day property is generally thought of as real estate and personal possessions, but in colonial times it had a wider meaning. Property consisted of whatever was owned. This included the body, mind and spirit of the person, as well as the opinions and dictates of one's conscience. A person's property rights began with the self and extended to ownership of externals. The value of property was rooted in the belief that human beings possess a God-given right to use their talents as nature intended. Individualism was part of it, but not in isolation, as it often is today. It was much more a spiritual and communal concept that stressed the individual's rights and obligations under God as a contributing member of society. Rather than freedom to evade responsibility or to demand special rights, property conferred the freedom to be productive and useful in a communal context. Governments were not needed to direct this process. Rather, they were needed to prevent the process from being interfered with by persons or groups, domestic or foreign, with designs on the property and livelihood of others.

This American idea was influenced by the Bible, later theological and philosophical ideas and by people like John Locke, the Enlightenment philosopher who saw government's role in these terms: Every person has the power to "preserve his property – that is, his life, liberty and estate – against the injuries and attempts of other men." He has the natural right to exercise this power on his own behalf, but because something one man considers his right may be regarded as an infringement by another, disputes arise that could lead to anarchy and social chaos. To prevent this, an arbitrating power becomes necessary. So men agree to give up enough of their personal power over property to ensure its preservation. They do this by putting it in the hands of a political society, which is formed by their consent. Thus, "the community comes to be umpire." As umpire, and not as dictator, government assumes its proper function (Locke, *2nd Treatise,* 56).

For the Founders, this was not just a philosophical, political or rationalistic principle. It was a deeply held religious belief as well, based on the human soul's need for creative activity and interaction. What upset early Americans was government interference with this natural process, as was the case with England. Property rights and individual liberty were closely intertwined concepts, and it was that notion of freedom that inspired the American Revolution and the creation of our constitutional form of government.

Our Founders were keenly aware of usurpations of property rights by England. In fact, they were so adamantly opposed to these intrusions that it can be said to be the principal cause of the Revolution. Our first formal statement on freedom, the Declaration of Independence, is mainly concerned with property rights. George III, it states, had gravely interfered with local governments, courts and elections; had sent swarms of bureaucrats and military to be quartered and supported by the people; had obstructed trade and imposed taxes without representation, and had "plundered our Seas, ravaged our Coasts, burnt our Towns, and destroyed the Lives of our People." These and other grievances were intrusions on property rights, and it was in this context that Americans demanded freedom.

NEW WORLD ORIGINS OF INDEPENDENCE:
ATTITUDES TOWARD PROPERTY RIGHTS

The connection between freedom and property rights was not new at the time of the Revolution. In fact, the idea goes back to biblical times. It was known to the original European settlers and put into practice soon after they came to America. In the early days, there were several attempts to establish workable forms of government in the colonies, but it was not long before respect for private property in some form was the norm. The history of these colonies in this regard is very interesting and deserves some attention. We can get a sense of the importance of property in the American understanding of freedom by reviewing the experiences of some of these settlements.

The Virginia Company

The first English colonies in America were settled under the authority of the Virginia Company, chartered by James I. Originally, the entire east coast north of Florida to Canada was called Virginia, in honor of Elizabeth, the Virgin Queen. Later, New England and other charters were created along the American coast. Expeditions were financed by investors looking for gold, silver and trade, but religion was also a priority, and in many cases the dominant factor.

Jamestown

The first English settlement to be established in the New World was Jamestown in 1606. It struggled and survived for a time, but was by no means as successful as some later colonies. Its history was filled with episodes of misery, starvation and Indian hostilities. More than once the Colony was nearly wiped out, but somehow endured and slowly grew. Tobacco became a viable crop, and there were times of relative peace and trade with the Indians.

One thing that changed Jamestown for the better was the institution of private property. Originally, most settlers were indentured servants who owned no land and shared resources in common. They were to receive land after seven years, but in the meantime felt little incentive to work. The King and company investors owned the land and resources, so the settlers felt there was no personal advantage in laboring for them or others in their group. People tended to lie back, waiting for others to provide food and necessities. The result was collective poverty and near starvation. John Smith had some success in establishing order in the Colony, but what really turned things around was the arrival of Sir Thomas Dale in 1611. He created an arrangement whereby each man got three acres to farm for himself. The Virginia Company's interest was reduced to one month's labor per year. These changes made a remarkable difference. In a few years the Colony was well supplied and doing reasonably well. Still, not all of its political and economic problems were solved, and the situation was compounded by more or less continual animosity between colonists and Indians. Finally, in 1624 the King dissolved the investors' company and made Jamestown a royal Colony, directly under government control. It remained as such until 1699, when Williamsburg replaced it as the capital.

The religion of these settlers was Anglican. In their charter, the King decreed that the primary purpose of the expedition was missionary, i.e., to spread the gospel to the Indians. Some think the profit motive was much more important, but this view may seriously underestimate the religious motive. King James I was a well educated man with a genuine interest in religion. It was he who commissioned the King James Version of the Bible, a monumental project which had a major impact in Europe and America. He and other authorities were deeply involved in religious matters in Europe and wanted Anglicanism spread in America.

Colonists were expected to be religious; church services at Jamestown became mandatory, with penalties for non-compliance. The fact that strict penalties were assigned suggests that the religious commitment of the colonists may not have been as vigorous as in other colonies, but this may be due to the difficult circumstances there. No doubt many were sincere worshippers. The fact is that they originated Anglicanism in the New World and began its spread throughout the region. By the time of the Revolution, it was the principal church in Virginia and other places in the South and a major influence on the culture there. Most Virginian Founders were active church-going members.

Jamestown is noteworthy for other reasons as well. Representative government in America was introduced there in 1619, with voting rights for property owners. It was not full participation because government authorities and investors retained significant veto powers, but the right to influence events through the vote was first established at Jamestown. An important element in this development was the connection between the vote and some form of property ownership, which remained a central feature of the American understanding of freedom for many years.

The concept of representation was initiated at Jamestown, but it did not extend to all. Among those disenfranchised were slaves, who came to the Colony by the accidental arrival of a Portuguese slave ship in 1619. Originally they may have been treated as indentured servants, but later history tells us that they became permanent slaves and part of the unfortunate development of the slave culture in America.

Plymouth

Other colonies had serious problems initially, but generally fared better than Jamestown. Shortly after that Colony was settled, a second Virginia Company expedition was formed. It was responsible for the Pilgrim migration to Plymouth in 1620. Company investors had economic interests, to be sure, as did some passengers on the Mayflower, but for most people aboard, the principal motivation of this venture was religious freedom.

Their journey from England to Holland and finally to the New World was a flight from religious and social oppression to freedom. Because they unintentionally landed where they did, they found themselves outside the jurisdiction of their Virginia charter. This meant that they were not under the authority of that charter or patent. Being Separatists anyway, i.e., not in communion with the Anglican Church either religiously or politically, they decided to establish their own form of government.

Their Mayflower Compact was written to establish consensus on how to organize and conduct themselves in this new situation. It stated their purpose – to advance the Christian faith, honor God and country and plant a colony – and spelled out some basic requirements for an orderly government. It also declared loyalty to the king, which had a special purpose. One of the reasons for writing the Compact as they did, wrote Governor William Bradford, was that some on the ship were not Pilgrims and were unruly. The fear was that, in the absence of the Virginia charter's authority, they would defy all authority unless everyone agreed to remain subjects of the king (Bradford, *Mayflower Compact*).

The form their little government took, and its eventual success, had long-lasting ramifications in this country. Their rejection of autocratic rule in favor of popular assent is familiar to us today. At first, elections were conducted by direct vote, but as the Colony grew this became unwieldy. So in 1638, representative elections began, anticipating the method adopted by the U.S. Constitution (Thwaites, 120-124).

The Pilgrims learned from hard experience with communal arrangements that life is much improved with private ownership. Under a system of common ownership required by European investors in the enterprise, the Plymouth Colony soon found itself in trouble. Like Jamestown, its very survival was in question due to lack of food, sickness and dissension among the members. But in 1623 Governor William Bradford addressed the problem by creating conditions of private ownership. He and the elders assigned a plot of land to each family, gave them seed corn and told them that whatever they produced on the land was theirs. Once given the incentive to work for themselves, the people began to produce surpluses and life in the Colony improved dramatically. In 1627 each family was given 20 acres and the Colony became independent by buying out the European investors. By 1643 there were 3000 inhabitants. Some moved on, but not because of poverty in Plymouth. According to Bradford, they moved away to find more land for cattle, improve their holdings and attain greater wealth.

Plymouth felt the effects of the emigration from the Colony, but, more than anything, Bradford seemed to lament the weak religious commitment and desire for wealth of those who left. Emigrants flowed out, he wrote, all around the Bay of Massachusetts, where they became rich raising corn and cattle. But there was a problem. In his words:

> For now as their stocks incresed...ther was no longer any holding them togeather, but now they must of necessitie goe to their great lots;...they must have land for plowing and tillage. And no man now thought he could live, except he had catle and a great deale of ground to keep them; all striving to increase their stocks. By which means they were scatered all over ye bay.... [And even worse] ye church must also be divided, and those yt had lived to long togeather in Christian and comfortable fellowship must now part and suffer many divisions. (*The Bradford Journal*)

Nonetheless, Plymouth continued to survive as an independent Colony until 1690-91, when it was joined to the larger Colony of Massachusetts.

The white man's immigration to the New World had a far-reaching negative effect on the Indians, as is well known. Not all relationships were negative, however, and the actual history of European-Indian engagements is a long and complex story. Against the popular view today that Europeans habitually invaded and forcibly displaced Indians are accounts of frequent negotiations, trade agreements and mutual respect for property. Regarding the Pilgrims, this may sound strange, given the fact that they first introduced themselves to the local Indians by shooting at them! The story is that Miles Standish and the landing party heard a "hideous and great crie" in the darkness and started firing. The Indians returned fire (with arrows) and the situation looked like the beginning of real trouble. But the next day everyone cooled off. It was explained that the Standish party thought they were firing at wolves, and non-violent negotiations began. The Plymouth colonists quickly established friendly relations with the local Indians for joint benefit.

The locals belonged to the Wampanoag tribe of Algonquin Indians who lived in the area along with other tribes. Some tribes were friendly but others engaged in ongoing hostilities with other tribes. The Plymouth tribe was subject to attacks of this kind, which gave them an incentive to avoid creating still another enemy. They were basically peaceful anyway, certainly more so than some other tribes, but mutual defense was an additional reason to consider the advantage of having these newcomers nearby.

In the first winter in Plymouth disease, hunger and lack of adequate housing nearly decimated the colonists. They lost half of the 102 Mayflower passengers who landed and may have lost many more without the help of the local tribe. These Indians already had encountered European traders and fishermen, and one, Squanto, had been in England and could speak the language. He proved invaluable to the newcomers, teaching them how to plant, fish and acquire other necessities. Massasoit, the sachem or chief, could also speak a bit of English. He made lasting treaties with these and other colonists that provided for respect for each others' people and property and for mutual defense against warlike tribes (*Pilgrims and Puritans*).

A 1649 deed granted a large tract of land to Miles Standish and two others named, who in turn bound themselves to provide the following consideration: "7 coates, 9 hatchets, 8 hoews, 20 knives, 4 moose skins, 10 ½ yds. of cotton." It was signed by Massasoit (here called Ousamequin) and by Standish and the others. The price seems low but it is not clear whether this was an outright sale or a permission to use the territory along with the Indians, as was the case with two other deeds

Massasoit granted. No doubt another factor was the desire of the Indians to cement good relations with their new allies (*The Bridgewater Deed*).

At any rate this and other agreements show that the colonists respected the property of these natives and did not steal it. The point is that while there are numerous examples in our history of Indian land being overrun and treaties being broken (on both sides), there are also many examples of legal negotiations and acknowledgement of property rights, especially in early times.

Guilford

Other English colonies made similar arrangements. In 1637, a contract was written that transferred land from a Connecticut tribe, the Manuncatuch, to European planters (colonists were known as planters and colonies as plantations). It named the English representatives and the Indian owner of the land, a squaw named Sachem. It provided:

> First, that Sachem Squaw is the sole possessor of the land in question,
> Second, that she, with consent of her tribe, is selling to the English planters the designated and mapped land,
> Third, that having received 12 each of coats, glasses, wompom, shoes, hachettes, stockings, hoes, hats, spoons and knives, as well as other items, she and the tribe are fully paid and satisfied.
> H. Whitfield signed for the planters; Sachem signed with her mark (a bow and arrow).

Both sides also promised to live in peace with each other and to make satisfaction for any harm done to the other if any should occur.

Relations between settlers and Indians could be tolerant, or even friendly, but, as in Plymouth, there was an additional motive for good relations. These Manuncatuch Indians were being pressured by unfriendly Pequot and Mohawk tribes and wanted closer ties with the English for their own safety. It is an early example of a deed that transferred private property from Indians to European settlers for the benefit of both.

In 1641 the same H. Whitfield arranged the purchase of adjacent land from an Indian named Weekwash, who had been given the property by the squaw Sachem Quillipiag. Later that year he bought land from Uncas, the Mohegan. That deed was signed by Uncas as well as by a squaw. These newly acquired lands could then be established as the Colony of Guilford. It was carefully laid out, with plots assigned to specific families, and like other colonies, had a strong religious character. In Guilford, lots were assigned specifically to Congregationalists and Puritans (Steiner, 28-33).

Massachusetts Bay

The Massachusetts Bay Colony was also a religious settlement, although it was founded as a trading company. Its most famous minister and leader was John Winthrop, who inspired many to come and make his Colony a "city on a hill', a beacon of light for the world. In time it became the largest of the New England colonies, absorbing Salem, Plymouth and others. Among its members, for a while, was Roger Williams, pastor of Salem in 1633. Among his "radical" ideas, which caused him to flee to Providence and found Rhode Island, were his opposition to church-state union, mandatory religious taxes and the notion that the English king had the right to grant American land. That right, he said, belonged to the Indians (Thwaites, 125-142). Unpopular at the time, some of these ideas became more acceptable later and influenced the thinking behind the American Revolution.

Connecticut had been part of Massachusetts until 1639, when it became independent. Its constitution proclaimed the principle of political authority deriving from the free consent of the people (Thwaites, 142-144). Long before our Founders' time, these colonies knew the importance of education for political freedom. Schools were established wherever possible for religious and civic instruction of the people, together with higher education for ministers, teachers and community leaders.

Regarding the Indians, relations could be friendly in some cases and antagonistic in others. Settlers found the Pequods to be as hostile to them as they were to the Manuncatuchs, which led to the Pequod War of 1637 and their defeat by Massachusetts and Connecticut colonists. But Indian-European relations were often quite good. The hostilities spoken of today were not commonplace but occurred sporadically in different areas over many years. The Indians were not a monolithic group. Many Indians lived in peace with colonists but fought with other tribes; some sided with the French in the French and Indian War while others backed England. Some tribes were welcoming; some were not. Some treaties were honored; some were not. When Lewis and Clark made their journey to the Pacific, they found a wide range of Indian cultures and attitudes. At length the Indians lost ground, but they always had defenders in America and still do.

Georgia

The last of the thirteen English colonies to be founded in America was Georgia. It was established in 1732, not as a trading settlement or a religious community, per se, but as a refuge for debtors and victims of religious persecution. James Oglethorpe, a wealthy and prominent member of Parliament, organized and led the expedition. He was supported by a sizeable number of Englishmen who knew the miserable plight of these people and wanted to assist them.

A charter, named in honor of George II, gave English rights to all settlers except Catholics. Its purpose was to aid the poor, protect persecuted Protestants and establish a military barrier between Carolina and Spanish Florida. It was carved out of South Carolina territory, but without objection and with considerable help from colonists there. One reason the new arrivals were welcomed was that they provided Carolina with military manpower against the Spaniards.

Oglethorpe established good relations with local Indians after an early skirmish, and contracted with them for land. Terms were satisfactory for both sides and conditions were peaceful. In fact, when Oglethorpe later went to England he brought the chief and some other Indians with him. They were well received and even met the King, who promised friendship, as did the Indians.

The problems this Colony encountered were not due to Indian hostility, as had been the case in Carolina, where serious conflicts had erupted earlier (Goodrich, *History of the U.S.*, "Carolina"). In Georgia, a major problem was that the immigrants were unwilling to work industriously. They came out of hard times and probably had defeatist attitudes to begin with, but also knew they were being supported by England. Of the thirteen, Georgia was the only Colony to receive direct financing from Parliament. The idea was to help the settlers get established, but critics said that this aid made the people less diligent and self-reliant.

Lack of motivation was a major reason Georgia did not prosper in the early days. Support from England reduced the desire to work, but possibly more important were the effects of land laws and the structure of the government. Land could be possessed only for a limited time and colonists had no voice in government affairs.

The Georgia charter was granted for 21 years, after which the territory was to revert to the Crown. Settlers could use landed property rent-free for 10 years, but with no say in the government and no guarantees of anything after the charter expired. Under these conditions the people had little incentive to work (Elson, Ch. IV, 93-97).

Oglethorpe wanted to produce an environment that fostered good morals. He brought the great preachers John Wesley and George Whitfield there for a time, but with limited success (Goodrich, *History of the U.S.*, "Georgia"). Also, there were moral laws forbidding slavery and rum. But many objected. It was said that slaves were needed to work the fields, as in neighboring Carolina, and rum was needed for use in trading. In time both laws were repealed, but conditions remained depressing. In 1752 the proprietors gave up and returned the charter to

England before it was scheduled to expire. It became a royal Colony with some local voting rights, but with a rapid increase in slavery. The English slave trade flourished and by 1776 almost half of the people were slaves.

Our Founders could draw important lessons from the unfortunate early history of Georgia. Oglethorpe had good intentions but the people did not respond well to their new circumstances. There were many factors involved in its slow development, but its restrictive laws regarding property and voting were especially troublesome. They became major concerns in all of the colonies by the time of the Revolution.

Other Colonial Influences on the Founders

Each of the English colonies in America has it own story, and each influenced the thinking of the Founders. Georgia was founded 125 years after Jamestown, yet it was still dealing with the same kinds of property and voting rights issues that earlier colonies had struggled with. One lesson to be learned from this is that these issues have deep and enduring roots which are not easily resolved.

It must be said, however, that some colonies handled these matters better than others. Maryland, for example, was an early Colony established by George Calvert (Lord Baltimore) and his son in 1634. Its charter ensured freedom for Catholics, which was unusual, and also for persecuted Puritans. The Toleration Act of 1649 extended religious freedom to all Christians. Laws were made by the proprietors *and* the settlers. No taxes could be levied without the consent of the people. Maryland was known for good government and friendly relations with the Indians. However, it did have problems with Virginia. Virginia strongly disputed Maryland's territorial boundaries and its religious freedoms. At one point its charter was abolished and Catholics were persecuted, a strange turn of events in a colony specifically founded to guarantee their religious rights. But the charter was later restored and Catholics were again accepted. John Carroll of Baltimore became the first Catholic bishop in America and his cousin, Charles Carroll, signed the Declaration of Independence. His brother, Daniel, signed the Constitution.

Another example of good government was Pennsylvania. William Penn, a Quaker, inherited the property from his father, who had received it from the King to settle a debt. He immediately made a successful treaty with the Leni Lenape Indians, who continued to remain friendly with the colonists. He sold land to immigrants at low prices to encourage them to come and get established. In 1682 Philadelphia was founded and a constitution, the Frame of Government, was created. Its inviting conditions drew immigrants from England, Ireland, Scotland, Holland, Germany, Sweden and other places (Elson, "Maryland" and "Pennsylvania").

Penn's *Charter of Privileges* in 1701 guaranteed freedom of religion for all who believed in One God. It created conditions for political representation of each county and emphasized that representatives be chosen based on their Virtue, Wisdom and Ability. It also ensured that on the death of a property owner the estate would go to his wife and family, thus keeping it in the hands of the family and preventing excessive accumulations by the wealthy. No doubt this was done in imitation of Old Testament laws designed for the same purpose (See *Family Property Rights* on pages 63-64).

The history of the English colonies set the stage for later developments in America. It is not difficult to see the relevance of that history to the desire for freedom at the time of the Revolution. Colonial experiments with private property rights, negotiated trades of land and goods, religious expression and limitations on government authority were part of the American story long before the events of 1776.

CHAPTER 2

The Founders' Views on Property Rights

> Wherever we cast our eyes, we see this truth, that property
> is the basis of power....Let the lands be possessed by
> people in fee-simple....Our jealousy of *trial by jury, the*
> *liberty of the press*, etc, is totally groundless. Such rights
> are inseparably connected with the *power and dignity* of
> the people, which rests on their *property.* (Noah Webster)

The Jamestown and Plymouth experiences, together with those
of other early American communities, strongly influenced later
colonists' approaches to workable political, economic and social arrangements. The most successful of these experiments were built
upon the belief that human freedom depends on the individual possession of property. But isolated self-interest was not part of this idea. It
was premised on a religious-moral conviction that people should be free
to use their God-given powers for the benefit of others as well as themselves. Our Founders inherited this notion and applied it in the formation of their new nation.

Noah Webster: On Property

Noah Webster is an excellent example of the early American spirit of freedom. He descended from William Bradford, Governor of the Plymouth Colony in the 1620's, and John Webster, Governor of Connecticut in the 1650's. He was born on his father's farm in Hartford in 1758 and entered Yale in 1774. During the War he belonged to the Connecticut militia, serving under his father's command. They were involved in the opposition against Burgoyne to prevent him from joining Clinton on the Hudson. After graduating from Yale, Webster became a teacher and was admitted to the Hartford law bar in 1781. He did legal work at various times in his life, served as a judge and in the Connecticut House of Representatives and as advisor at the Constitutional Convention. He was a founder of Amherst College and became a member of the General Court of Massachusetts. He had a family of eight children and lived to age 85.

Today Noah Webster is known mainly as an educator. He spent much of his life promoting the kind of education that emphasized American culture and the moral character necessary for citizens of the new Republic. He wrote spelling and grammar books that were widely used in schools for over 100 years and is probably best known for his dictionary, still used in revised form.

He also had much to say about property. He believed that ownership of land gives citizens the power to live freely. In view of the egregious usurpations of property in Europe and elsewhere, he strongly advocated laws that encouraged ownership, but also laws that prevented the excessive accumulation of property by any individual or family, which has the effect of denying ownership to the poor.

Webster believed that our nation could survive as a newly formed constitutional republic only if its founding principles endured, and for that to happen two things were needed on a wide scale: private property and general education. Without them, too many citizens would remain poor and ignorant, their votes would be meaningless or dangerous, and the nation would soon return to some form of pre-revolutionary dictatorship, or to anarchy. For him, and for most of our Founders, these two ingredients were absolutely essential for the success of the American experiment.

He was a strong supporter of Washington and of federalism at a time when suspicion of government power was high, given the colonial experience with the government of England. Webster was very much aware of the real and potential abuses of government, but also of the necessity of having a government to protect the natural rights of citizens. Thus he argued for strong, but very limited, public authority to act in those interests. In this, and in many other ways, he represents the thinking of those Americans who opted for freedom from English political coercion and for the rights and obligations of independence.

English history had taught Webster that the age-old battle for liberty from the time of the Magna Charta could not be achieved without a wide distribution of property among the people. It never was achieved in terms of landed property, most of which remained in the hands of the nobility, although over time it was partially attained by virtue of the personal property acquired through commerce and manufacturing. The lesson he learned was that property is the basis of liberty because it confers power, and liberty exists in direct proportion to the property held by each individual. America had to learn this lesson and, regarding real property, ensure that no man be able to gain control over a large territory. Thus, "the laborious and saving, who are generally the best citizens, will possess each his share of property and power, and thus the balance of wealth and power will continue where it is, in the body of the people. A general and tolerably equal distribution of landed property is the whole basis of national freedom" (Webster, *Leading Principles*).

Commerce indeed aided the quest for freedom, but even there ownership of land continued to play a vital role. In New England, Webster noticed that small estates had allowed large numbers of people to possess real property, which required them to labor and be industrious, giving them pride in their accomplishments and their independence. This made them more socially responsible and agreeable generally, but also gave them the power to resist any encroachments on their property or person.

Webster recognized certain dangers with this arrangement. One was that people could be beguiled by slick politicians who preyed on their desire for independence by convincing them that greedy individuals were intent on gaining control of their property. The accusing politicians would appear to be innocent, upstanding citizens, but in fact could be the most unqualified men for authority in the community. But the fear of losing property rights might cause citizens to vote them into office, thereby putting governments in the hands of the weakest or most devious citizens.

Another danger was that a wide-scale division of land could result in parcels becoming so small that the owner could not make it profitable. If a father, for example, owned a sizeable plot of land and divided it among several sons as inheritance, each divided plot might not support a viable farm. If the new owner and others in similar circumstances had to sell, more prosperous citizens could buy land cheaply and thereby acquire large holdings, thus defeating the original purpose of distribution. This was not yet a major problem, but a likely future one. Webster did not seem to know how to deal with it, except to say that he hoped the solution would be determined by wise statesmen, based on the situation at the time.

Another serious challenge to freedom was the institution of slavery. Webster considered slavery a great evil and publicly opposed it. Since most slaveholders considered slaves as property, it was difficult to convince them of its repugnance on moral grounds alone. Belief in the rights of private property was too strongly ingrained. So Webster appealed to economic as well as moral arguments. In 1793 he wrote *Effects of Slavery on Morals and Industry*, which outlined his moral position and also gave detailed financial estimates on the actual cost of owning slaves. He concluded that slave labor was more costly and less productive than free labor and that it was in the best interests of owners to release their slaves and hire free workers.

He was a member of the Connecticut Society for the Promotion of Freedom, an abolitionist group that he wrote and spoke for, and wrote articles for *The Minerva,* a New York newspaper. There he made similar arguments on slavery, one of which contrasted the wealth of the North with the poverty of the South, claiming the difference was due to the predominance of slavery in the South. Yet he did not try to carry his campaign into the South, believing, as he told one of his daughters, that Northerners had no more right to impose their views on Southerners than for them to do so in the North.

Another area of interest to Webster was intellectual property. In his day there was little legal protection for authors against plagiarism and copying of books for resale. He was keenly aware of this problem, since his popular schoolbooks were targets. He worked for many years to establish copyright laws in America, going to each state and to the federal government. Success finally came in 1790, when Washington signed the first national copyright law. But Webster continued working on this issue until a better law was passed that extended the protected period.

Webster was not entirely certain that America could survive challenges of the kind he foresaw, although he obviously believed in the possibility. A real threat was that widely held ownership of property, especially land, would diminish, and with it the spirit of the Revolution. In the absence of landed property, could the benefits of commerce and manufacturing suffice to maintain the desire for personal and political independence? Of that he was not sure. He said that every government reflects the condition and spirit of the people in it, and if Americans were to lose the principles and spirit of a free government, they would quickly lose the form (Webster, *On the Divizions of Property*). We may wonder today, now that commerce, money and services are such important sources of wealth, whether that early American spirit of freedom burns as brightly as it once did.

Benjamin Rush: On Human Rights

On politics and freedom, Benjamin Rush was of the same mind as Webster. He was the son of a gunsmith in Philadelphia, who died when he was six, and of a mother who made ends meet by running a grocery store. He attended an academy at age eight, and then Princeton, where he graduated at age fifteen. He then went to Edinburgh for his M.D. and did further study in London and Paris. He returned to teach chemistry and medicine at what is now the University of Pennsylvania, and became well-known and respected for his medical innovations. He taught thousands of medical students, who established practices across America. In 1837 some of them created the highly regarded Rush medical school in Chicago.

Rush was an ardent advocate of republican reforms in America. He encouraged Thomas Paine to write *Common Sense* and helped publish it. He was active in the Continental Congress, signed the Declaration of Independence and was Surgeon-General for a time in Washington's army during the war. He later served in the administrations of John Adams, Thomas Jefferson and James Madison. He and James Wilson were principal authors of the Pennsylvania constitution in 1789-90. His many involvements over the years proved that he was a thoroughbred revolutionary with strong beliefs in the human potential for self-rule.

His ideas on freedom and property are found in the Declaration of Independence, which he helped formulate. Property rights, freedom of expression and the dignity of man were ideals close to his heart. Although he was born into a slave-owner's family, and owned at least one slave himself, he gradually began to realize that his revolutionary ideas of freedom and property should be extended to the slave population. Even as a young man he wrote articles condemning slavery, and he later helped form the Pennsylvania Abolition Society. He also freed his own slave. Rush was known for providing medical treatment to the black community, and to all the poor. He supported the African Church and risked contracting yellow fever by continually giving medical services to blacks during an epidemic in 1793.

Rush was one of the strongest believers in education of his time. He thought it was critical for moral development and the understanding of republicanism, as well as for grasping the importance of property rights. He promoted free public education in Philadelphia because of his conviction that the republic could not survive without it. He also tried to advance the cause of liberty by encouraging harmony between the strong-willed political leaders of the day such as Adams and Jefferson. They did agree on the meaning and importance of property rights, but their ideas on the role of the central government differed, as did their views on the Alien and Sedition Act and on aid to France during its revolution. Once close friends and collaborators, their later disagreements caused them to part ways for many years. Rush believed that the influence of both men had been fundamental in the creation of the new republic and was still needed. It was he who found a way to bring these two giants of the Revolution back together again.

Benjamin Franklin: On Taxation and Representation

Whereas Webster and Rush understood liberty basically in the same way, Benjamin Franklin presents a more complex revolutionary figure. He seemed to genuinely love England, its traditions and benefits to mankind, as well as the opportunities it offered to people like himself. He wanted reforms, but for a long time was not interested in separation and tried in his own way to prevent it.

Initially, Franklin's views on property rights were strongest in regard to taxation. The problem had been that large tracts of land in the colonies were owned by "Proprietors," who had been given the land by the Crown. In Franklin's day the major Proprietors in Pennsylvania were descendants of William Penn. He had been sent to England to get Thomas Penn, William's heir, to pay taxes on this land, which was being defended by the locals from the Indians and the French. It became a drawn-out affair that went from one delay to another.

Franklin was slow to respond to calls for separation, possibly because of his hope for eventual favorable treatment on the Penn affair, as well as his hope for a land grant in Ohio. He also wanted to protect his position as Postmaster. He was in England when the Stamp Act was established, which placed a tax on documents, papers and legal instruments in the colonies. Franklin thought this was an infringement on colonial rights, but only a minor one. While in England he counseled appeasement and obedience, not realizing how upsetting this tax was to most colonists. This led to a colonial rejection of the tax, and also of Franklin, who was blamed for promoting it. The uprisings in America over this were so strong that Franklin's house in Philadelphia was threatened and probably would have been destroyed if not for the armed resistance of his wife and friends. Franklin tried to calm the waters by writing letters proclaiming his disapproval of the tax, and finally by making an argument for repeal directly to the Parliament. When the tax was repealed, Franklin's reputation was restored.

The next thing Parliament did was to create new taxes on a number of imports, including tea. This again caused so much dissension that these duties were rescinded, except for the tax on tea. It was thought that this small tax would be accepted since the new price of tea, including the tax, was made so low that it cost less than it did before the tax was imposed. The idea was to establish the principle that England had the right to tax imports. This too was rejected. Tea sat on the docks or rotted in warehouses in Boston. Finally the symbolic right to tax was met with the symbolic Boston Tea Party, which did little physical damage apart from the loss of the tea, but sent the message that colonists would pay no tax without representation.

Franklin disapproved of the Tea Party and continued to support English-American union even as colonial discontent grew stronger. More uprisings occurred due to increased unrest over England's attempts to tax without colonial consent. Franklin argued that these taxes would be acceptable only if colonists were represented in Parliament, where they could have a say in such matters. Parliament refused. He surmised that most of the American rage was directed against the Parliament, and if loyalty to the King could be preserved, separation could be prevented.

In an attempt to shift the blame away from the King, Franklin released some private letters of Governor Hutchinson of Massachusetts that implicated Hutchinson in attempts to tax and further subdue the colonies. When it was revealed that Franklin was involved with the publication of these letters, Parliament was outraged. In a public session where he stood silently for an hour, he was repeatedly attacked and humiliated as a liar, thief, lecher and rebel for exposing the Hutchinson letters.

It was at this point that Franklin, angered and disgraced, changed course and actually did become a rebel. He stayed on in England for some time, even though there was talk of more charges being brought against him over the Hutchinson affair. But he finally left after it became obvious that his efforts to curtail Parliament's hard line against the colonies had failed, as had his case against the Proprietors. This also ended his attempts to obtain a land grant in Ohio and a royal appointment for himself. On top of all that, he lost his position as Postmaster in the colonies.

Franklin gave up his quest for lenient British treatment in America and for personal favors or appointments to office, although he had already helped his son become Governor of New Jersey. He became a full-fledged separationist, bitterly resenting his treatment in England and also bitterly resenting his son's refusal to join him in rebellion. They became estranged and never reconciled.

It was then that Franklin became a zealous advocate of independence. He influenced the delegates to the Continental Congresses, helped write the Declaration of Independence and the Constitution, and spent years in France promoting the American cause. He is given credit for convincing France to enter the war, although that did not happen until the American army showed that it was not going to collapse and could win at least some battles.

The tax issue, which became a major cause of rebellion, was a property issue. Franklin seemed slow to pick up the implications of this. He understood the injustice of taxation without representation, but initially thought it was not an issue serious enough to foment violent defiance. But once his personal reputation was trashed in England, it must have become clear to him that the tax dispute was more than a monetary problem. It involved not only property but also the dignity of the owners of property. England's uncompromising attitude toward the colonists showed a level of disrespect that deeply insulted them. For Franklin, a very wealthy man, the amount of the taxes was not the issue, which was no doubt true for most colonists. It was the principle of subservience that inflamed the people. They considered themselves the equals of all Englishmen, but the Crown's arrogant imposition of taxes and clumsy handling of local issues showed disrespect for the colonists' private property, which included their personal human rights.

Regarding private property rights, Franklin strongly believed that ownership of property should be based on self-reliance and hard work. This was a long-held moral position for him, and it reflected his own life experiences. It also corresponded with his distaste for the special privileges assumed by the upper classes. But he also felt that the well-to-do should help the truly needy as long as it did not make them dependent and lazy (Isaacson, 55-60, 89-92, 474).

On the subject of the most dependent, the slaves, he had a more difficult time forming a solid opinion. As in the case of his good friend Benjamin Rush, he eventually began to apply the idea of American freedom to the black community. At one time he owned a few slaves, one of whom ran away while in England. Franklin, however, did not pursue him even though he knew his whereabouts. He later helped establish schools for the blacks and joined Rush in the Pennsylvania Abolition Society. In 1790 he offered an abolition petition to Congress, which did not pass. The idea of slaves as property was still too embedded to allow for emancipation. In his will, Franklin gave his house and other property to his daughter, Sally Bache, and her husband, with the stipulation that they free their slave, Bob. They did, but Bob could not adjust to his new life and returned, asking to be made a slave again. The Baches refused to do that, but let him live in their house the rest of his life (Isaacson, 472).

George Washington: On the Defense of Property

The life of our first President exemplifies the American spirit of freedom and its connection with property rights. By the age of seventeen he had established himself as a competent surveyor and was already buying unclaimed land. Later, he inherited Mount Vernon from his half-brother Lawrence. Over the years he expanded the site from 2000 to 8000 acres. He also acquired land in what is now West Virginia and the District of Columbia. As a farmer he initiated changes that helped the estate financially. He switched from cultivating tobacco to wheat as the main crop, experimented with new plants, crop rotation, tools and fertilizers. He built a flour milling and commercial fishing business, and at one time had one of the largest whisky distilleries in America.

Washington was a man who valued property and what can be done with it and, like his contemporaries, deeply resented British interference. He was not the first to advocate separation, but eventually became one of its strongest supporters. When the time came, he accepted his commission as commander of America's army and fought against enormous odds for freedom. His military defeats were humiliating, so much so that many on both sides thought the rebellion had failed, and all that remained was for Washington to surrender. But Washington did not surrender and would not quit, and in the end achieved an unlikely and surprising victory.

After the war Washington came to be regarded as America's greatest hero, not only because he refused to surrender and somehow stumbled to victory, with vital help from the French, but also because of his personal character. He was admired by all for his integrity, bravery and honesty, and for his steadfast convictions about the American cause. He could have been proclaimed king, or have remained President for life, but chose to give up power and retire after two terms. He believed in limited powers for himself and for all government officials. In his mind no man was indispensable and power must not be concentrated in the hands of one or a few. This attitude is consistent with his fear of excessive government interference with property rights.

Washington held slaves, as did many others of his time who considered them as property. Today we look upon this as an egregious injustice and also as hypocritical for revolutionaries fighting for freedom and equality. In hindsight, we see this much more clearly than they did. We see slavery as the great evil it is, but we have not grown up in a slave culture. Slavery had existed throughout human history, and slave traders in Europe had institutionalized it in the American colonies. People of the time were accustomed to slavery, and most of them probably simply accepted it as part of life. In his early days Washington was no doubt one of them.

Washington became more sensitive to the issue as an adult. After the Revolution he remarked that only by rooting out slavery could the Union survive. He became outraged by auctions where slaves were bought and sold like cattle. He signed legislation prohibiting slavery in the Northwest Territory. Later he said: "There is not a man alive who wishes more sincerely than I do to see some plan adopted for the abolition [of slavery]." He began to see it as a political issue, one that could eventually destroy the Union, and as a moral issue for a nation dedicated to justice. It also affected him personally, and although he was not willing or able to do so while alive, in his will he provided for his slaves' freedom after his wife's death. However, she freed them soon after he died.

A Note on Slavery

There were abolitionists at that time, some being slave-owners themselves, but they could not carry the day. Webster, Rush, John Adams and his son, John Quincy, and many others opposed slavery. Washington's good friend Alexander Hamilton, for example, belonged to New York's Manumission Society for many years. Members ran a school for one hundred black children and worked to mitigate or end slavery altogether. They were known for defending free blacks from slave masters from other states who tried to kidnap them from New York (Chernow, 580-1). Hamilton also strongly objected to the mistreatment of Indians. He was a supporter and trustee of an upstate school for Indians and whites which was later named Hamilton College in his honor (Chernow, 338).

There were many attempts to help the slaves in those days. By 1795 Rhode Island, Vermont, Massachusetts, New Hampshire, Pennsylvania and Connecticut were making plans to free them or already had decided to do so. Some slaves were freed, but abolitionist efforts often were strongly opposed.

It is important to recognize the conditions of the time regarding slavery. The point is not to defend slavery in any way, but to see it in context because the very fact that some Founders held slaves causes many today to dismiss their contributions altogether. But it is easy to be an abolitionist now that slavery has been abolished. It was not so easy then. During the revolutionary period, unity among the colonies in the War against England was threatened by controversies over slavery. As the abolitionist movement grew, opposition also grew. In the 1830's antagonisms became increasingly violent. Abolitionist William L. Garrison was physically attacked and the hall where his group met in Philadelphia was burned to the ground. Lewis Tappan in New York had his house destroyed. Frederic Douglass and many others were aggressively harassed. John Brown's tragedy was an abolitionist affair. We are accustomed today to see slavery as a racist issue, but then it was very much an economic issue. Southerners believed the plantation economy of the South would collapse without it, and the unemployed in the North feared competition for jobs by freed slaves. One of the best indications of the depth of the problem is the ferocity of the Civil War. Freeing the slaves required a monumental effort that cost hundred of thousands of lives, uncounted injuries and disabilities, broken homes and enormous financial outlays.

The slave trade had been supported and encouraged by England since early colonial days and was a primary reason for the development of the plantation economy in America. It became so entrenched that even abolitionists could see that emancipation would create enormous upheaval. Not only would the economy suffer severely, but the prospects for most of the freed slaves would be bleak. Where would they go? What would they do? As slaves they were valued as property, but as free people they had no economic value for former owners. This could open the door to even greater forms of exploitation. In New Orleans, for example, owners refused to send their slaves into the bogs for building projects because of the high danger of malaria and other diseases. The Irish, however, were poor and desperate for work. Having no property value to anyone but themselves, they were considered expendable and were given the work slaves were not allowed to do. Among abolitionists, there was a concern that as freemen, slaves could have been treated as badly as or even worse than these Irish and other "worthless" poor. The early American history of slavery is a dark and complicated episode in our past. It was gravely evil, but a problem not easily solved. As we later learned, it took one of the most vicious and bloody war in our history to solve it, and even then not completely.

John Adams: On Property as a Sacred Right

Our second president was a vigorous American reformer and one of the first to openly advocate independence from England. In this he followed in the footsteps of his older cousin, Samuel, known as the "Father of the American Revolution." England regarded Boston as the hotbed of rebellion, led by John Hancock and especially by Sam Adams. Cousin John was soon in their company, demanding the rights of free men and convincing other colonists to do the same (Puls, 65, 131-132). He became an unwavering force in pursuing separation and a chief reason that it succeeded.

John's thoughts on property and the role of government are revealed in his comments on the Massachusetts Constitution. When asked for advice on establishing the voting franchise, he advised the General Court to be very careful in establishing the requirements. Some members wanted to extend the vote to practically everyone. Although Adams believed that power always follows property, he said that those without property lack the necessary stake in society to make responsible voting decisions (Adams, *Letter to Sullivan*). Giving the vote to everyone without limit would repeat the mistake the Romans had made. They learned from bitter experience that widespread voting privileges lead not to a stronger nation but to social unrest and upheaval. With the vote, the Roman majority was able to pass "agrarian laws," which took property away from the rightful owners and gave it to those with no property. But rather than creating equality and a more just society, these laws increased instability and public irresponsibility. He and other Founders did not believe in getting something for nothing and regarded these Roman laws as important causes of the fall of the Empire (Smith, *John Adams*, 258-260).

Adams firmly believed in prosperity, but not if provided by confiscation of other people's property. It is why he insisted that voters have a tangible stake in society to ensure responsible voting. Private property must be respected at all costs. If everyone, regardless of circumstances, had the vote:

> [It] would not be long before … pretexts [would] be invented by degrees, to countenance the majority in dividing all the property among them, or at least, in sharing it equally with its present possessors. Debts would be abolished first; taxes laid heavy on the rich, and not at all on the others; and at last a downright equal division of everything be demanded, and voted. What would be the consequence of this? The idle, the vicious, the intemperate, would …sell and spend all their share, and then demand a new division of those who purchased from them. The moment the idea is admitted into society, that property is not as sacred as the laws of God, and that there is not a force of law and public justice to protect it, anarchy and tyranny commence. If 'Thou shalt not covet,' and 'Thou

shalt not steal,' were not commandments of Heaven, they must be made inviolable precepts in every society, before it can be civilized or made free". (Adams, *Defence of the Constitutions*)

His solution was not to raise an army to defend landowners from the poor, but to make the possibility of ownership as widely available as possible. Even very small estates qualified, so that most citizens could vote. He thought laws should encourage ownership of property, which is a badge of honor for the individual and a safeguard against irresponsibility. Knowing that tax laws and regulations applied to their own possessions as well as to the rich made all voters more cautious and accountable.

Property rights were sacred but there was a limit on what should be considered property. Among the Americans of the revolutionary period, Adams was in the minority in his views on slavery. He strongly opposed it and backed up his conviction by never owning a slave. He said the labor costs on his farm would have been much less had he owned slaves, but he refused to do so. He simply did not believe that some human beings should be considered the property of other human beings.

Thomas Jefferson: On Property as a Natural Right

As principal author, Thomas Jefferson's ideas on freedom are enshrined in the Declaration of Independence. His writings there and other places reflect the influence of western religion, philosophy and history, and also his own personal experience. He knew first-hand of England's abuses of property rights in America, and he also witnessed similar abuses in France. He told of one incident that happened while on a walk near a French village. He asked a local woman what people there did for a living. She told him that most of the people in her village were unemployed. She explained that it was because the land in the area was owned by a few nobles who reserved it for their sport hunting and prevented the locals from using or working it for any purpose. To show his appreciation for the information Jefferson gave the woman a few coins. She was so amazed by his generosity that he concluded that this was probably the first time anyone had ever given her anything. Witnessing the dismal plight of these peasants caused him to write to Madison that America must never allow such accumulations of land and wealth because of the consequences for the people at large. Property is a natural right, he said, one that provides special benefits to those who own it and enjoy the product of their labor. It is in the interest of both individuals and the nation that land be distributed widely among the people because "the small landholders are the most precious part of the state."

Like Webster, Jefferson regarded agriculture and the rural way of life as sources of the American zeal for freedom. In his *Notes on the State of Virginia,* he wrote: "Those who labour in the earth are the chosen people of God, if ever he had a chosen people, whose breasts he has made his peculiar deposit for substantial and genuine virtue. It is the focus in which he keeps alive that sacred fire, which otherwise might escape from the face of the earth."

Later, in 1787, he wrote a letter to Madison that combined the two ingredients he believed necessary for American freedom:

> I think our governments will remain virtuous for many centuries; as long as they are chiefly agricultural; and this will be as long as there shall be vacant lands in any part of America. When they get piled upon one another in large cities, as in Europe, they will become corrupt as in Europe. Above all things I hope the education of the common people will be attended to; convinced that on their good sense we may rely with the most security for the preservation of a due degree of liberty. (*Letter to Madison,* 1787)

On the question of slaves as property, Jefferson seemed to have serious reservations. He owned many, but appeared to regret it. He was not able to bring himself to free his own slaves, possibly out of self-interest, but also out of concern for their future away from his protection. Today he is roundly condemned as a freedom-loving hypocrite, but his treatment of his own slaves, and their regard for him, and his efforts in behalf of all slaves, suggest that he had a genuine interest in their well-being and even their freedom. He tried several times without success to have slavery mitigated or abolished in Virginia, and also in other parts of America. In the Declaration of Independence, he wanted to include a condemnation of England for the evils of slavery in the colonies but was outvoted. He did succeed in preventing its spread in the Northwest Territory.

James Madison: On Property as a Natural, God-given Right

Land has traditionally been the foundation of wealth, but as already mentioned, these leaders considered property to be more than land. James Madison defined property as land, merchandise, money and any other tangibles a person owned – and also as the free expression of one's thoughts and abilities. As he, Locke and others said, each person has a property in himself. This includes personal opinions, the right to express them and to live according to them as long as they do not infringe on others' similar rights. Both tangible and intangible forms of property and their associated rights should be protected. Madison's view was that the purpose of government is to "secure to every man whatever is his own."

The Declaration of Independence expresses this outlook. It is due to "the Laws of Nature and Nature's God" that all men are entitled to certain unalienable rights, including "Life, Liberty and the Pursuit of Happiness - That to secure these Rights, Governments are instituted among Men, deriving their just Powers from the Consent of the Governed...." This text clearly states the signers' view that these rights are given by God and not by government. The problem today is that secularists seek to downplay or even deny the religious underpinnings of our political history, a view that has serious implications for our understanding of the structure and purpose of American government.

A Note on Secularism

A distinction is in order here. A "secularist" is one who promotes secularism, which purposely ignores, excludes or actively opposes religious expression, whereas a "secular" person is simply occupied with temporal matters and is not overtly religious (Webster's Third New International Dictionary). The latter is not a problem for constitutional government. Most of daily life could be termed "secular." In our system, freedom of conscience supersedes all religious conformities. Individuals can believe or not believe whatever they wish, provided they do not infringe on others' rights. Jefferson and Madison were leading figures establishing this precedent. Secularists, however, are not merely non-religious. They object to religious expression by anyone in public places and actively oppose it. To them, church-state separation means that religion has no place in government, schools or other public forums. But the exclusion of the religious viewpoint has implications that go beyond public display issues. Secularism also ignores religious ideas about the nature and capabilities of human beings. The problem for democratic society is that if people, especially children, are denied knowledge of their natural God-given powers and abilities as taught by western religion, they are less likely to believe in their capability to live freely. That, in turn, can make them more amenable to authoritarian government rule.

The secularist stance creates new and conflicting interpretations of early American views on church-state separation and the role of the citizen in society. Church-state issues, as currently understood, heavily favor secularist approaches even though they are not in keeping with early American constitutional thinking. Early American attitudes toward human intelligence and capabilities, and the corresponding purpose of government, are rooted in biblical and philosophical concepts that acknowledge human weakness, but also respect man's natural ability to live without coercive external authority.

Self-respect

"A man's character emerges in the building and ordering of his house" (Weaver, 146). Against the secularist distrust of human strengths is this affirmation of self-reliance and self-respect. The "house," of course, is not only a building, but anything that employs physical, mental and spiritual powers for productive purposes. The saying acknowledges the natural impulse to be active in useful enterprises, i.e., to work for something meaningful. It points to the reason that dictatorship tries to suppress independent ingenuity and self-direction. It also shows why unemployment is more than a money problem. It is also a psychological and spiritual problem.

The American attitude toward property and freedom is built on a long tradition of respect for the dignity of human beings, beginning with the biblical teaching on man as the image of God. "In the image of God he created them. Male and female he created them". Humans are made to be creative and productive as God is in his Creation. Adam's first task was to care for the Garden, and then, outside the Garden, to work the land and make it fruitful. Although fallen, he still had the necessity and the capacity to be industrious and productive. This meant that he had to have access to the means of production. Traditionally, this has meant unencumbered use of land, possessions and money through ownership or some form of lease or contract. Madison and his colleagues knew that the inability of many to acquire these tools of production has been the cause of enormous suffering and social disruption throughout the ages.

It is in this context that the evil of slavery must be considered. Madison grew up on a slave plantation in Virginia, and, like others, probably thought little about it early on. It was simply assumed that slaves were the property of their owners, as had been the case for thousands of years. However, Madison did not believe in mistreating them, and later showed considerable interest in mitigating or abolishing slavery.

Although he can be faulted for never freeing his own, he had a reputation for treating them humanely. Yet, as well as they may have been treated, they were still slaves.

Madison was one of our greatest leaders in the pursuit of freedom, but we must acknowledge that he was not a purist when it came to slavery. There are indications that he was troubled, perhaps deeply so, about campaigning for freedom while holding slaves himself, but like most slave holders, he did not free them.

Madison belonged to a group dedicated to freeing slaves and returning them to Africa or relocating them to the far west, away from slave territory. He gave money for this project and argued for emancipation in the Continental Congress, but little was accomplished in that age of institutionalized slavery. Slaves were property and owners had property rights, an idea so entrenched that equal treatment of them was probably beyond the imagination of most slave-owners.

Courage and the Revolutionary Spirit

Lest we dismiss the Founders on all counts because of slavery, we should measure that failing against the contributions they did make toward freedom. One of them is their courage in pursuing separation from England. The ideas held by the makers of this nation were acted upon at the risk of losing the property they already had, including their slaves, as well as their families and their own lives. It is interesting to reflect on this as we consider the depth of their dedication to freedom. Most were wealthy and prominent in their communities and had much to lose by defying England. They knew this, yet put everything on the line. They won the War, but many were personally ruined.

Signers of the Declaration of Independence faced special perils. The British made extra efforts to hunt them in particular, and many paid a heavy price:

Carter Braxton, one of the wealthiest men in Virginia, loaned money and ships to the war effort and lost almost everything. His ships were sunk or confiscated by the British and most of his plantations were destroyed. He never recovered financially.

Abraham Clark of New Jersey had two sons who were officers in the military. They were captured by the British and confined in the Jersey, a notorious prison ship known for rampant disease and death of prisoners. One son was intentionally being starved to death until he was finally released under heavy pressure and threats of retaliation on British prisoners.

John Hart of New Jersey lived on the run in forests and caves for over a year. He returned to find his property destroyed, his wife dead and his thirteen children missing.

George Clymer of Pennsylvania had his home, library and belongings completely destroyed by the British.

William Ellery of Rhode Island saw his property and home burned.

Thomas Nelson used his money to finance the attack at Yorktown. During the campaign, his home was being used by Cornwallis as his headquarters, yet he urged Washington to fire on it, which Washington did. Nelson lost a fortune during the War, and instead of receiving gratitude he was accused of authorizing supply purchases without advice from the state council. Washington defended him and he was finally exonerated in 1781. He served in Congress without pay and never regained his wealth.

The British destroyed the New York home and large library of Francis Lewis and jailed his wife. She was so mistreated that she lost her health and died a year or so after being released. Mr. Lewis spent the rest of his life in poverty (*Signers of the Declaration of Independence*; Goodrich, *Lives of the Signers*).

The stories of these and other revolutionaries did not end happily. It was hard enough for those who were more fortunate. They not only had to manage to get through the War, but then to engage in the extremely difficult task of forming a new government. Opinions differed and arguments were heated as the new nation struggled to create a political structure that would survive. The remarkable thing is that all of these obstacles were foreseen. The willingness of the revolutionaries to stand up and fight against such odds shows the depth of their commitment to the cause of freedom.

Why did they rebel, knowing the risks as they did? We may assume that more was involved than the specific grievances listed in the Declaration of Independence. Underlying these complaints was their determination to live as free men according to each one's conscience. For them, personal wealth and favored circumstances could not compensate for fundamental infringements on the right to think and act as independent human beings. They saw that when a king or any outside power can dictate the use of one's property, including personal expression and behavior, basic rights are being violated that are worth fighting for. They believed that government exists to ensure that these rights are protected from foreign and domestic aggressors. When the government itself became the aggressor, revolution erupted.

Freedom of Conscience

The American belief was that the power of government was not to be used to control land and dictate personal opinion, but rather to prevent some people from overrunning the rights of others. They saw that governments can serve this function by protecting property rights. One of these rights is freedom to express opinions and live according to one's conscience, which includes freedom of religion. Madison repeatedly brought this truth to the surface. What he and Jefferson actually thought about the religious beliefs and practices of their day is not easy to determine, but they certainly were not the atheists and despisers of religion portrayed by enemies in their time or by anti-religionists today. These two in particular fought for separation of church and state, but not because they wanted to destroy religion. Their aim was to prevent governments from establishing state religions. They abhorred the idea of states imposing taxes for church support and of churchmen having legal authority to demand conformity to any specific church teaching. But this does not mean they wanted freedom *from* religion. They only wanted freedom to express religious beliefs, or no belief, as one sees fit. Thus, atheists have rights too, but not the right to forbid or intrude on the religious expression of others. It is doubtful that Madison and Jefferson ever conceived of the possibility of religious expression being denied as it is in schools and public venues today. They surely would have had no part in trying to undermine the religious notion of human dignity that underlies the early American understanding of freedom.

CHAPTER 3

American Religion and the Spirit of Freedom: On Property Rights

Recently, an atheist in Florida sued the Christians for discrimination because they have Easter and Christmas as special holidays, whereas atheists have none. After hearing the charges, the judge, exasperated and annoyed that such a case could come to trial, slammed down his gavel and dismissed the case. The atheist's lawyer objected because the atheist's claim was true – he had no special day. The judge denied that. He did have a special day, said the judge – April Fool's Day – and then quoted the Psalm, "The fool says in his heart, 'there is no god'."

T he judge treated the atheist's case with ridicule, or humor, depending on how one sees it, but it may not have been because he had conservative religious views. More likely he was upset that such a complaint could even arise in an American court. It showed how far some have wandered from the original idea of American liberty. The atheist and his lawyer, rather than trying to be controversial, actually may have believed that this was a case of discrimination. They may have been unaware, as many citizens are, that this nation was founded by people who promoted a free religious culture (Moore, 79). It was formed by church members, for the most part, and by application of Christian moral tenets, but no one was to be persecuted because of religious beliefs. Each person had the right to live by the dictates of conscience, whether Christian or not.

The early American worldview was philosophical, historical and, lest we forget, biblical. We can easily underestimate the influence of that inheritance today, having moved so far from the religious atmosphere of earlier times. The Founders' debt to natural law philosophy is better known than their knowledge of the Bible and Judeo-Christian teaching, although the latter played a vital role in the development of the American idea of freedom.

Education in those days, whether formal or home-based, concentrated on biblical teaching, and church influences were widespread. If we want to understand the American concept of freedom, we must acknowledge that fact. This does not mean that everyone must be a church member or even believe in God. It simply means that our history should be respected for what it is, and religion is a big part of it, beginning with the recurring biblical theme of freedom from oppression. It takes many forms, physical and spiritual, based literally or figuratively on the story of the Hebrews' exodus from Egypt to the Promised Land.

THE BIBLE

The Exodus Motif: From Slavery to Freedom

The idea of freedom in the Old Testament is founded on the Exodus story. It tells of the Hebrew escape from Egypt and return to the ancestral land to the North where Abraham and his family had lived. It was there that the people hoped to find freedom. Freedom in the Promised Land was spiritual, based on adherence to God's Law, and material, founded on possession and use of personal property, land and its resources.

Ownership of property made the people free, but, as was repeatedly taught, only if they lived in accordance with God's will.

The Old Testament (The Hebrew Bible)

Abraham: Why Owning Land Mattered

to This Wandering Aramaean

Abraham, the father of the Hebrew people, predates the Egyptian Exodus but his life exemplifies the Exodus theme. He and his descendants were known as wandering Aramaeans who left their native place in search of the land that God had promised. As a nomad, Abraham traveled widely, settling in various places to care for his flocks and family. But this was always a temporary possession of land, lasting only as long as each season provided pasture for the animals. It was apparently a satisfactory lifestyle, since he became wealthy doing it, but when his wife Sara died, Genesis tells us that he was determined to acquire a permanent location to bury her. There were religious and family reasons for doing this. It was as if he wanted a tangible, earthly anchor in the land God had shown him to honor his wife and to establish a permanent burial ground for his family. In his own way he was making a down payment on the Promised Land later inherited by his progeny.

Genesis records a lively and humorous story of the negotiations between him and Ephron, the Hittite owner of the field and cave that Abraham wanted. It teaches a lesson about the deep-seated human desire for ownership of property. In the presence of the town council, Abraham offers to buy the property, called Machpelah. Ephron, however, offers it as a gift to Abraham. This polite gesture may have been an act of generosity, but more likely was part of the traditional bargaining process. It showed his willingness to give or sell the land, which was a way to publicly proclaim his financial strength. In any event, Abraham did not want a donation; he wanted unqualified full ownership.

One can almost picture the scene of them discussing the transaction. In the style of Mideast bargaining their back and forth dialogue continues until Ephron finally mentions a figure in an offhand way, as if to say, "What is such a trifle among friends? It is not worth even discussing." But Abraham immediately recognizes this as Ephron's asking price and he agrees. Through this public ritual Abraham formally gained permanent possession of the property in the presence of witnesses (Genesis 23). This was an important episode in his life because it gave him long-term ownership of the property. He was later buried there himself, as were Isaac and Jacob, as well as their wives (Genesis 49:29f. and 50:12f.).

Burying the dead in a specific place was a sacred and natural act in those days and still is. In earlier ages and in early America people had churchyards and other marked places to provide permanent memorials for deceased family members. Today there seems to be more willingness to scatter ashes and leave no marker, but it is still commonplace to buy cemetery plots in perpetuity, with deeds and property rights attached to them. It reinforces a basic human need to be connected with the land and point to the place where the deceased returned to the earth from which they came (Genesis 3:19).

Moses: The Law and Property Rights

> If "Thou shalt no covet" and "Thou shalt not steal" were not commandments of Heaven, they must be made inviolable precepts in every society, before it can be civilized or made free. (John Adams)

After Abraham, famine caused his son Jacob to abandon the homeland and settle in Egypt, where his people prospered because his son, Joseph, had become a high official there. But the book of Exodus tells us that another Pharaoh eventually arose, who knew nothing of Joseph and his people and began oppressing them. By the time of Moses they were essentially slaves. It was he who aroused the people's desire to escape by revealing God's promise to take them to the land they had left. Belief in this promise was tested often once they left Egypt. The people discovered that freedom *from* the Pharaoh was only the beginning of their journey. They still had to find freedom *to* the Promised Land. Life was hard during the Exodus and there were rebellions, but hope in the promise never died. In time it was fulfilled when the people settled in the land of their ancestors.

The Pilgrims were mindful of this story and thought of their passage to America as another exodus from oppression to freedom. Like the Hebrews, they dared to reject their rulers and move out. Both groups endured hostilities and struggled to find the freedom they sought. The Hebrews wandered through the desert; the Pilgrims went to Holland and then sailed to America. Death-dealing events accompanied both migrations. Many died but those who survived established themselves under a covenant, first at Sinai and then at Plymouth, with rules of conduct and laws of justice. The laws at Plymouth were reminiscent of those found in Moses' Law.

The commandments that Moses received on Mount Sinai had much to say about property rights. We find prohibitions against stealing and coveting the belongings of others in the Ten Commandments (Exodus 20), and many specific rules protecting real and personal property (Exodus 21-22). Many were taken for granted in early America.

The book of Leviticus contains an interesting description of what was called the "Jubilee Year," or the fiftieth year, which spells out rules for asset transfers among Israelites. The purpose of these rules was to ensure the long-term retention within the family of property "sold" or given to another to settle debts. Such transactions were not intended to be final. Permanent ownership was to remain in the original family. These agreements were more like leases than sales, with the original owner or his descendants recovering the property after a specified time had passed. If the time until the Jubilee Year was short, the price for the property would be less, and if long, the price would be greater. This rule applied to both land and personal possessions, including the indentured servitude of a person who "sold" himself to another to pay a debt. The object of this arrangement was to keep landed property in the hands of the ancestral families and to prevent slavery among Israelites. Thus the rich could not gradually take over possession of large tracts of land, leaving others in poverty, nor could they imperil the freedom of individuals by enslaving poor Israelites (Leviticus 25).

The fact that the Jubilee Year's provisions were preserved and taught to later generations demonstrates the Israelites' respect for freedom, although history does not tell us that this law was scrupulously observed. Its intent, however, reflects the fundamental attitude of the people and their Exodus experience. The basic premise was that land and the people belonged to God and not to any human ruler or owner. The Israelites were tenants rather than absolute owners. They were to use their God-given property with respect and justice toward their neighbors.

The same spirit is found in the "sabbatical year" laws. Some of these referred to land that was to be left uncultivated every seventh year. The weekly Sabbath provided rest for the people; the seventh year Sabbath gave rest for the land (Exodus 23:10, Deuteronomy 15:1, Leviticus 25:2). Today we would probably call these environmental precepts designed to protect the land from exploitation. Another feature of these laws was their application to people owing debts, which were to be forgiven after seven years. And there were laws giving slaves the right to be freed if they wanted to leave after seven years (Exodus 21:2, Deuteronomy 15:12).

Americans inherited and accepted the value of these laws. They did not simply duplicate them literally, but they established legal principles designed to provide equal treatment of property owners and to avoid excessive concentrations of land or other forms of wealth. The Constitution's separation and enumeration of powers, the rights of the accused, the Bill of Rights and other provisions reflect the spirit of these safeguards.

Family Property Rights

Another indication of Israel's respect for private property is found in a law regarding rights of inheritance. The Bible tells a story of a man who died without leaving a son to inherit his property. Inheritance typically passed on to males in the family but in this case there were no males, so the property could then be acquired by outsiders. However, the man did have five daughters. Foreseeing their possible loss, they came to Moses to ask that they be allowed to inherit the property. Moses judged that their plea was just because these daughters were closest of kin and should have prior rights. Allowing them to have the property would prevent the inheritance from being removed from their father's clan. It therefore became a law that in the absence of a son, inheritance should be conveyed to surviving daughters in order to keep property in the family (Numbers 27). To further support these aims, daughters inheriting property were required to marry within their clan to ensure that each tribe would retain its ancestral territory (Numbers 36).

Another law in this regard required the brother of a deceased husband to marry his widow if the brothers owned property in common. This "levirate" marriage allowed the name of the dead brother to live on through children born of the marriage, and also kept his property within the clan's boundaries (Deuteronomy 25).

Related to this law is the story of Ruth, a foreigner from neighboring Moab, whose husband was an Israelite from Judah. After he died without children, Ruth refused to abandon her mother-in-law, Naomi, who had also lost her husband and remaining son. Naomi was poor and needed to sell the family property, but she also wanted to help Ruth find a husband. She arranged things so that a close relative knew of this situation. Boaz, the relative, responded by agreeing to marry her and buy the property. A legal formality in the presence of witnesses allowed Boaz to assert his claim. The hereditary custom was thereby preserved. The child born of this union was raised in the name of the deceased husband, and the land remained in his clan. The child's name was Obed, who became the father of Jesse, the father of King David (Ruth 4).

The spirit of these laws was revealed much later at Jamestown and among the Pilgrims, and still later by other colonists. Property was assigned to families, with exclusive rights to own and use it, and to pass it down to their progeny. Excessive concentration was not an issue then, although there was growing awareness of its danger. By the time of the Revolution it was a major problem regarding the King's holdings, and Webster, Jefferson and others were concerned about it for future Americans. Our founding documents recognized this danger, especially regarding government control of land and the rights of individuals.

Property Rights under the Kings

> The History of the present King of Great-Britain is a History of repeated Injuries and Usurpations, all having in direct Object the Establishment of an absolute Tyranny over these States. (Declaration of Independence)

The Declaration of Independence presents George III as an abusive ruler who did not deserve allegiance. It was a risky assertion, not only because of the power of the king to retaliate, but also because of the long-held belief that kings were chosen by God. It was difficult to convince people to overthrow rulers who were thought to have their position by divine appointment.

One reason abusive kings of the past managed to retain power was this notion of the divine right of kings. The Founders had to persuade those so inclined that George III had no divine right to abuse his authority. He was simply one of many kings known to history who, with or without divine rights, had unjustly oppressed their subjects. The Bible supported this view, which no doubt helped the Founders make their case. It tells of the divine appointment of some kings, but not all, and not necessarily for their entire reign. Israel's first king, Saul, is an example of God's choice and anointment through Samuel, and later rejection (1 Samuel). The Bible records abundant examples of kings who trampled on the rights of others, but also of some who respected those rights.

Regarding private property, the Bible teaches that these rights were not to be violated, even by the kings. A story about David illustrates this. David, who had by this time assumed considerable power, wished to offer a sacrifice because of a plague. The owner of a threshing floor offered to give him the land, animals and everything necessary for this, but David insisted on paying full price, even though the owner was not an Israelite. It was not right, he said, to offer sacrifices to God by using property that cost nothing (1 Chronicles 21-22). Although he could have simply taken the land or seized it by force, he acquired it by contractual negotiation. His example was a sacrificial gesture, but it also upheld the right of property ownership, even of foreigners, and taught a lesson in justice. It bore fruit when his son Solomon later built the Temple there.

Reading the history of Israel after Solomon's kingdom split into two parts might leave the impression that no one had much freedom of any kind, including the kings. It is a history full of violence, war and brutality, yet there is also evidence of respect for property rights within the tribes. Brute force did not always rule the day. Omri, for example, battled his way into power and could have taken his subjects' property at will. But after gaining the kingship by winning a civil war, he decided to build a city. Rather than simply confiscating land, he bought and paid for it and even named it after the seller. It was Samaria, which became the major city in the Northern Kingdom (1Kings 16).

Later, his son, King Ahab, decided he wanted a vineyard that was near his property. He offered full price for it but the owner, Naboth, refused to sell because it would remove it from his ancestral heritage. Ahab did not try to seize the property himself, but his wife, Jezebel, cooked up a scheme to have Naboth killed for supposedly insulting God and the king. The treachery worked, and Ahab then was able to take possession of the land. The prophet Elijah nearly lost his life for severely condemning Ahab and Jezebel for this and other crimes against people and property. He foretold the total demise of Ahab's family because of these outrages, which later came true (1 Kings 21).

Israel's prophets continually opposed the obstruction of property rights by the powerful. Amos was a simple shepherd, but he had a keen sense of God's justice. He saw the oppression of the poor by the rich and publicly reacted to it. He spoke God's word, vehemently condemning their evil practices:

> For three crimes of Israel, and for four, I will not revoke my word; because they sell the just man for silver, and the poor man for a pair of sandals.
>
> They trample the heads of the weak into the dust of the earth, and force the lowly out of the way. (Amos 2: 6-7)

Hosea was another early prophet who saw all too clearly the dangerous path Israel was on. Widespread idolatry had turned the people away from the Law of Moses. Idolatrous worship involved more than reverent gestures toward statues. It included adulterous and orgiastic rituals, child sacrifice and worship of money and power, shown by the unchecked corruption of merchants, judges, government officials, and kings. Hosea compared Israel's covenant to the close relationship of a marriage, saying that the people's idolatry was like marital infidelity. The harm caused is irreparable. The message of Hosea and other prophets was not optimistic: the nation was headed toward collapse.

After the fall of the Northern Kingdom to the Assyrians, Isaiah, Micah and other prophets took up the same message in the Southern Kingdom. Isaiah publicly condemned the power plays of the wealthy to strip away the rights of the powerless for their own benefit:

> Woe to you who join house to house, who connect field with field, till no room remains, and you are left to dwell alone in the midst of the land!

He warned that there would be a price to pay for these injustices:

Many houses shall be in ruins, large ones and fine,

with no one to live in them. (Isaiah 5: 8-9)

The prophets' main complaint concerned Israel's rejection of the Mosaic covenant. Idolatry led to unwise treaties with foreigners and grievous acts of injustice against fellow Israelites. Many prophetic teaching concerned crimes against property, both real and personal. Jeremiah had the courage to attack King Jehoiakim for this:

Woe to him who builds his house on wrong, his terraces on injustice; who works his neighbor without pay, and gives him no wages....

Your eyes and heart are set on nothing except on your own gain, on shedding blood, on practicing oppression and extortion. (Jeremiah 22: 13-17)

In most cases, Israel's prophets failed to convince the people of their wrong-doing, at least in part, and many failed completely. Their message was clear, but the people usually paid little attention. But during the times when the people did accept the prophets' teachings, Israel prospered. The message, given over and over, was that Israel could succeed if the Covenant was obeyed. The fact that Israel survived at all shows that there were some who did live by the Covenant. Even the Babylonian Exile did not cause the nation to die out.

There are countless references to freedom in the Bible, many referring directly to property rights. Even when not honored, as was often the case, these teachings gave hope to the people. Israel endured countless catastrophes in its history. If it were not for Israel's fundamental belief in the Exodus motif – the possibility of finding a life beyond the crushing coercion and injustice so common in the ancient world – there might be no biblical record, or any record, of their hopes and struggles for freedom.

The same idea applied in America. The Founders believed that applying the rules of conduct described in the Bible and reflected in the Constitution would guarantee the strength of the nation and ensure its future. It explains their vital interest in schools, moral education and general knowledge of property rights.

The New Testament

Material and Spiritual Freedom

The New Testament continues the Exodus theme, but in a somewhat different context. Although many New Testament teachings are found in the Old Testament, we can notice a shift in emphasis from material and political forms of freedom toward personal and interior freedom. This is highlighted by the Gospels' account of Jesus' spiritual journey, culminating in his passion, death and resurrection. Because this model of freedom concerns personal spirituality more than material property rights and political emancipation, many have concluded that the Gospels are indifferent or even antagonistic toward such things. It is true that some of Jesus' sayings seem to show little regard for material things:

> "No man can serve two masters….You cannot give yourself to God and money" (Mt. 6:24), "Sell what you have and give alms. Get purses for yourselves that do not wear out, a never-failing treasure with the Lord…. Wherever your treasure lies, there your heart will be." (Luke 12: 33-34)

These texts are often used to condemn materialism, but they cannot mean that material things have no value. There is little freedom of any kind without the ability to conduct daily life in accordance with basic human requirements. Looking further into Jesus' teachings, this becomes apparent. Material concerns are obvious in his many physical cures and approvals of almsgiving, and also in some of his dealings with rich people.

Is Having Wealth Evil?

We see in Jesus' teaching warnings against greed and possessiveness, but not condemnations of people for being rich. He dined with them, had some as his disciples and praised some for their use of money. We may safely conclude that His opinion of people was not based on their wealth or lack of it.

Zacchaeus was a tax collector and a wealthy man. When Jesus saw him on the road near Jericho, He told him he wanted to stay at his house. Zacchaeus was delighted, but others were not because tax collectors were despised in Israel. Zacchaeus defended himself, saying:

> I give half my belongings, Lord, to the poor. If I have defrauded anyone in the least, I pay him back fourfold. Jesus said to him,

> Today salvation has come to this house, because this is what it means to be a son of Abraham. (Luke 19: 8-9)

Nicodemus was a Pharisee member of the Sanhedrin. He and Joseph of Arimathea, another Sanhedrin member, became disciples of Jesus and are known for arranging His burial (John 19). These men had wealth and prestige, but are not depicted as immoral in any way. Other wealthy personages in the New Testament are also approved. Among them is the rich man Jesus loved for his fidelity to the Commandments. Even though he would not sell his property and follow Jesus, the fact that he kept the Commandments was enough for Jesus to love him (Mark 10:21). Also approved is the scribe, a man of influence, who understood and agreed with Jesus' interpretation of the Commandments. To him Jesus says, "You are not far from the reign of God." (Mark 12:34). The parables of the Good Samaritan (Luke 10) and the father of the Prodigal Son (Luke 15) also present favorable pictures of men of wealth.

The first Christians in Jerusalem lived a communal life, but recognized the property rights of others even in their own community. Ananias and Sapphira sold property and announced that they gave all of the proceeds to the Church. Peter, however, knew they had secretly retained some. He confronted them, not for keeping some back, but for lying about it. "Was [the property] not yours so long as it remained unsold? Even when you sold it, was not the money still yours?....You have lied not to men but to God!" (Acts 5:4). They both died from shame and fear, but their sin was deception, not ownership of property.

Money is property, but is having it good or evil? Does it rightfully belong to the rich or is it the product of greed? In 1766 a law prohibiting the export of grain to England created excesses and lowered the price in America. This affected farm income but some thought this was justified because farmers lived too well anyway. One farmer, thought to be richer than he deserved to be, gave an expensive wedding for his daughter. This proved, it was said, that he could well afford the loss of grain income. He objected:

> I am one of that class of people that feeds you all, and at present is abus'd by you all; in short I am a Farmer.... Are we Farmers the only people to be grudged the profits of honest labor? And why?
>
> [Have our opponents] never read that precept in the good book, *Thou shalt not muzzle the mouth of the ox that treadeth out the corn*; or [do they] think us less worthy of good living than our oxen? (Benjamin Franklin)

Franklin was a wealthy man who lived very well, but he did not horde his money or use it to exploit the poor. He gave generously to churches, schools, the needy and to the young. He had the highest regard for Jesus' moral teaching and did not believe it condemned wealth. He was not alone in this. It was the attitude of many of the Founders.

Work, Property and Human Dignity

Where did the Founders get the idea that work and property ownership were related to human dignity? We may be sure it did not come solely from European sources because it is a basic tenet of the Bible. A good example is found in Paul's writings.

Paul of Tarsus believed in working for a living and having sufficient funds to be self-reliant. He advised his disciples to work as he did and support themselves rather than depend on the largess of others. This had become a problem with some disciples who believed that Christian freedom meant being free to do nothing. Paul made a point of denying that interpretation of his message, saying that those with property were not obliged to give to those who refused to care for themselves. Charity was necessary only for those in real need. To the Thessalonians he wrote:

> We did not live lives of disorder when we were among you, nor depend on anyone for food. Rather we worked day and night, laboring to the point of exhaustion so as not to impose on any of you....Indeed, when we were with you we used to lay down the rule that anyone who would not work should not eat. (2 Thessalonians 3: 7-10)

The major emphasis on freedom in the Gospels and Epistles concerns spiritual freedom – freedom under God, freedom from sin and the freedom of love – but this does not annul values established in the Old Testament. The above examples show that the New Testament viewpoint on freedom has a material component that involves care of the physical person and respect for each person's property. The body, mind and spirit are not dissociated from each other in this life, which is why private property is an important foundation for human freedom.

Biblical freedom is built on the principle of human beings as God's children. If we ask where Madison and others got the idea of the person as property, the answer is surely here. Every biblical story, prayer, psalm, poem and historical account teaches something about human capabilities for good or evil, most of which pertain to treatment of other human beings. The Bible is filled with exhortations to act in accordance with God's law and its concern for persons, understood in the early days as fellow Hebrews, then later also as strangers and finally as everyone, including enemies. As the Law protects physical property, it also protects personal property, including the soul and spirit of every person.

To separate the American notion of freedom from religion, as is so often done today, is to seriously misunderstand our beginnings and the values that underlie our principles of government. The connection between freedom and property rights has a long history. Early Americans did not invent it, but they were especially dedicated to preserving and fostering it.

CHAPTER 4

Contemporary Ideas

Regarding the Supreme Court's 2005 Kelo decision which upheld the city of New London's right to take private property for another private use:

Any property may now be taken for the benefit of another private party, but the fallout from this decision will not be random. The beneficiaries are likely to be those citizens with disproportionate influence and power in the political process, including large corporations and development firms. As for the victims, the government now has license to transfer property from those with fewer resources to those with more. The Founders cannot have intended this perverse result. (Dissenting Opinion of Justice O'Connor)

History records the events of the eighteenth century American Revolution, but the story does not end there. As Benjamin Rush said after the War, the Revolution is not over; it continues as citizens learn to function in their new republic. It continues yet today, although with less energy than before. Over time the zeal for the freedom wrought by property rights has weakened in this country and the intrusive power of government has strengthened. There are many examples of this.

Misuse of the Power of Eminent Domain

Kelo

Consider the recent experience of Susette Kelo, who lived in the Fort Trumbull section of New London, Connecticut. It included 115 private properties and some families had been there for generations. It was not a blighted area at all, but since Pfizer was developing a $300 million research center there, the city decided to use Pfizer as a magnet for further economic growth in the area. It therefore gave the power of eminent domain to a private development company to clear the land and prepare the site for private commercial use, including a hotel, some marinas, restaurants and retail stores. It was thought that this would improve New London's tax base.

Since Kelo and others refused to give up their properties, the development company initiated condemnation proceedings against them in November 2000. The owners then sued, citing the Taking Clause of the Fifth Amendment, which states, "No person…shall be deprived of life, liberty or property, without due process of law; nor shall private property be taken for public use without just compensation." Their principal objection was that in this case the power of eminent domain was being used to transfer property from private owners to other private owners, instead of to the public for public use, as was its historical usage.

The case reached the U.S. Supreme Court in 2004 and was decided in favor of the city in June 2005. Justice Steven's majority opinion claimed that the term "public use" in the Fifth Amendment no longer meant "use by the public," as it had since our founding, but now, in recent times, means "public purpose." It was decided that economic revitalization and increased tax revenue serve a public purpose, which makes the taking of private property for another private use legitimate (*Kelo*).

This decision created an uproar in the nation as people realized its implications. It was seen that practically any project could qualify as meeting the "public purpose" criterion, and under this rule no one's home or possessions would be safe from government confiscation (Arnn, 2).

Columbia

The Kelo episode is only one of many other attempts to use eminent domain to take private property for non-public use. Columbia University tried to take seventeen acres of private land for what it thought was a better use, but was stopped by the New York Appellate Court in late 2009. The Court claimed that the argument for seizure of this property was "sophistry" and unconstitutional. That opinion, however, was appealed and overturned by a higher state court. Then that decision was appealed to the U.S. Supreme Court, which declined to hear it, thereby allowing the takeover to proceed. Columbia is prepared to spend $6.3 billion on this project (Stohr).

Had the Court taken the case, it would have been interesting to see how it handled it. Given its current makeup, would it rule in favor of Columbia, explicitly or implicitly reaffirming Kelo and causing even more controversy? In effect, by declining the case, it did rule for Columbia, but in a way that did not require addressing the Kelo precedent. Also, would it have considered the accuracy of the blight designation of the property? The reason for condemnation of the property was that it was blighted, but there were strong rebuttals by plaintiffs on this point, partly based on Columbia's neglect of deteriorated property it already owned in the area. Also, the objectivity of the environmental study was disputed because of the reporting company's connections with state agencies and its seemingly biased track record. There is also a question about the proposed public use of the land. The purpose of the taking is supposedly educational, but Columbia has commercial research enterprises that likely would be located there (Bullock, A11; Chaban).

Questions remain. Kelo raised a great stir over confiscation of peoples' homes, but in the Columbia case commercial property was at issue. Would the case have been handled differently had it included residential properties? How was the blight designation arrived at and how was the report scrutinized? Will the new use actually be "educational" in the sense of being beneficial to the public, or will it be a center for specialized training and research of benefit mostly to the university itself? It should be noted that Columbia has a history of extensive involvement with research projects that produce license fee income for the University, amounting to well over $100 million each year. In 2009, it was second in the nation in research-related income, and executed 51 licenses and 202 patent applications (AUTM). Will this acquisition be devoted to that commercial "mission," and if so, how does general education benefit, if at all?

The project is proceeding, but not without difficulties. People are still objecting to this so-called "educational expansion," and there have been a number of on-the-job mishaps. A demolition company with a questionable background has been fired after two deaths and injuries to others. As of May 2012, Columbia and its contractors have been served with 59 building code violations and 13 stop-work orders (Durkin).

Wyoming

Another eminent domain dispute involves a plan to create pathways for electrical transmission lines for wind turbines in Wyoming. These "collector lines" would run through agricultural property, creating a hardship for farmers using the land. Not only that, compensation for the land would likely be valued for its agricultural worth, but condemned to allow for higher valued industrial use. It would provide a one-time payment for permanent easements that would generate continuing income. The estimated income would be $266,000 per turbine over 20 years vs. a one-time payment of $10,000 for the easement. There has been so much opposition to this that the state legislature issued a moratorium on eminent domain use by wind developers and has extended it until 2013 to further study this problem (Bleizeffer; Casper Star-Tribune).

These are the kinds of complications that come up with eminent domain issues. Some applications are legitimate, but when there is a dispute, the process heavily favors the government entities over the landowners. When private property is condemned for future private use, the stakes are especially high. The fact that this can happen at all shows that conditions have changed since earlier times, when the property rights of individuals were more valued and guarded.

The aftermath of Kelo reveals signs of a still healthy, although weakened, desire for independence in this country. Before being demolished, Kelo's little pink house was moved to the center of New London and set up as a monument. Tours are given there telling the story of the Fort Trumbull tragedy. On the front porch is a sign that reads, "Not for Sale". Kelo and others continue to give talks about the abuse of eminent domain, and by 2010, forty-three states had passed laws limiting its use. Seven state high courts have ruled in subsequent cases in favor of private owners against eminent domain for private use. Workshops are being given around the country to inform people on this subject, resulting in the defeat of numerous attempts to impose eminent domain for local projects. In one case, the city of San Pablo, California tried to use eminent domain for a project comprising 90 percent of the city. The outrage was so great that the city council had to abandon the project. In the end it actually voted to ban eminent domain for private development (Walsh).

As for the Kelo affair at Fort Trumbull, the city's efforts have not fared well. In November 2009, Pfizer announced it was pulling out of the plan for the research center, and the city has been unable to find investors to develop the area. Weeds cover most of the targeted area and nothing has been built. So instead of increased tax revenue, New London has lost the revenue it once had when the houses were there.

Regulation and Confiscation

The Kelo case is a blatant example of taking, but there are many other less obvious examples. Among the most damaging are ill-advised zoning and building codes that serve little purpose other than to allow government agencies to control the use of people's property. In these cases the typical rationalization for interference is that society and the environment must be protected against unwise use of property. This means that "society" (i.e., government officials) gets to decide how owners can use their property. Physical confiscation is not necessary because regulation can accomplish similar effects, but in a less obvious manner.

An example of this is regulation of trees on private land. Some cities have such strict rules that an owner cannot remove a tree threatening to fall and do damage without going through a time-consuming and costly permit process. In one case in California, roots of a large tree close to a home were undermining the foundation. Also, bulky branches would fall periodically endangering anyone near the front porch. Still, to avoid a heavy fine, a permit was required to remove it. This required preparation of a plot plan of the entire property, submission of an arborist's opinion and payment of a fee. The city then sent five letters to neighbors asking them to respond if they objected to the removal for any reason. After a time, with no objection forthcoming, the case was sent to the city council for a vote. Following an affirmative vote, five more letters were sent to neighbors giving them one last chance to object. More time passed. Finally, with no objections being received, the city issued the permit, with the provision that three trees be planted on the property to replace the one lost.

This is a relatively minor example of a much larger problem. Some states and localities have stricter rules than others, but interference of this kind can happen anywhere. People have had huge trees fall and destroy their homes because of denials or delays in getting permits. In building projects, grading permits, set-backs, variances, code upgrades, inspections and a host of other requirements drive up costs and delay or prevent completion. In almost every case, a good reason can be given for the existence of each requirement, and in theory each can be defended. Saving trees, for instance, is a good thing, but not when they become severe dangers to people and property. The problem is that codes and other regulations are often interpreted so arbitrarily and unreasonably that people lose control of their property and cannot avoid dangerous and unwarranted conditions.

Some regulations are beneficial to the community but others are so restrictive, complicated and expensive that owners are unable to do reasonable things with their property. Citizens and companies have gone bankrupt due to government fees, penalties and delays on projects that should have been approved, or, if not, denied in a timely manner before thousands and sometimes millions of dollars have been spent on permit requirements.

A related problem is the government-sanctioned unequal treatment of property-owners. The cost of compliance with regulations often prevents individual homeowners from building or making additions and improvements to their property. Yet giant developers, armed with a phalanx of lawyers and deep pockets, can sometimes manage to plow through the governmental red tape and build many houses similar to those that single homeowners are unable to build or improve. This is more than unfortunate in a nation dedicated to the promise of equal rights for all citizens.

Another problem is that companies are being swamped with overly aggressive regulations that impede their ability to do business. The issue is particularly acute for small businesses that do not have the resources to deal with all the paperwork, reports, fees and interruptions imposed by government agencies. Besides land use obstructions, there are cumbersome financial reporting requirements. Many have pointed to Sarbanes-Oxley as particularly troublesome. Environmental rules can also be major problems when they are applied improperly to business enterprises. No doubt laws like these are well-intentioned, but they can become so onerous that a struggling business may not be able to compete. There are many causes of business failure, and excessive government meddling is one of them.

What is the cause of America's loss of private property rights? The boldness of government infringements on these rights would not have been tolerated in earlier times. Why now? One clue has already been given long ago by Noah Webster, who wondered what would become of our Republic if commerce, merchandise and money were to supersede land as the primary form of property. Jefferson, Adams and others also understood the link between land and freedom. They worried about the values and interests that people would have if they lost their connection with the soil.

When we think of freedom today, we must recognize that early American expressions of freedom came forth from a predominately agricultural society, whereas today the dominant economy is industrial, informational and service oriented. Does this change our understanding of freedom? Possibly it does to the extent that industrialization creates large concentrations of people in factory and city locations, as do other large-group economic enterprises. The Founders wondered about the impact of that on freedom. But even if people are willing to submit to the demands of bulky and powerful organizations, there is still an underlying human desire for the personal freedoms so well articulated by the writers of the Declaration of Independence and the Constitution. No doubt that will continue to be the case as long as this nation retains the western and particularly American spirit of freedom, which is grounded on more than possession of land. There is also the belief that humans are capable of responsible self-direction.

More important than land ownership rights may be the shift from a religious culture toward secularism (See *Note on Secularism* on page 51-52). Secularism takes God out of the picture, as well as the biblical teaching associated with personal responsibility. We are left with explanations and suggestions about ethical behavior which lack the depth and vigor of traditional morality. As the original composition of American society slowly slips away, the constitutional form of government, based on individual rights and responsibilities, slips with it. If this trend continues, it becomes increasingly difficult to imagine a future nation having a constitutional government worth much to the individual, or having one at all. Part II deals with this in more detail.

If the American form of constitutional government is to survive, more must be done to protect private property. Some of the problems with unwanted government intrusion can be somewhat self-correcting, as we see with the reaction to the Kelo decision, but mainly it comes down to the decision of voters and those genuinely interested in their communities. People will vote and act wisely, however, only when they know and understand what is really happening to their freedoms. Schools could contribute to this awareness by teaching students the historical meaning of freedom and its connection with property rights. Freedom can then be seen as more than unencumbered individualism. It will be recognized as the fundamental right to use both personal and real property as one sees fit, without harming others, and in a way that contributes to the well-being of both the individual and the community. In that context, government's role is to defend private property, rather than to grant, bestow or control it.

PART II
GENERAL EDUCATION

How General Education Promotes Property Rights

I wish that those who complain of the great decay of Christian piety and virtue everywhere and of learning and acquired improvements in the gentry of this generation would consider how to retrieve them in the next. This I am sure, that if the foundation of it be not laid in the education and principling of the youth, all other endeavors will be in vain....'Tis virtue then, direct virtue, which is the hard and valuable part to be aimed at in education. (John Locke)

CHAPTER 5

The Founders' Views on Education

Government takes its form very much from the character
of the people to be governed; and a republican or free
government, necessarily springs from the state of society,
manners and property in the United States. No other form
is proper for the country.... (Noah Webster)

Much can be explained about how we live by what we believe to be true. Some behaviors are spontaneous, such as
sudden emotional impulses or responses to survival dan-
gers, and others are dictated by biological and physical characteristics.
Still, it seems evident that human acts are largely conditioned by ideas
we have learned. The ideas we have in our heads and the way we think
about them have a huge effect on how we live. It is true that humans
have internal intuitive sources of knowledge, but we also receive a great
deal of information from the external world. If we pay attention, we can
sense how the mind feeds upon these external stimuli and processes
them into ideas. Over time, they become part of our worldview. Thus,
little children will form their notion of the world based upon innate
knowledge, but also upon life experiences and the teachings of parents,

instructors, peers and other social influences. This process continues throughout life, as ideas are refined, developed or changed.

This is why education is so important and why parents and others are concerned about it. In America, we have a tradition regarding education's value that goes back to colonial days, and far beyond that. Our Founders were fervent believers in it, and based fundamental faith in it in their design for the Republic. They believed that we are creatures of God, who has given us intelligence and the means to act as free beings, which means we need not have recourse to rulers like George III or any other dictator. We are capable of self-rule by our God-given faculties, which provide us with the possibility of living under a democratic form of government. The Founders were influenced by biblical teaching, Greek and Roman thought, and by later theologians and philosophers such as John Locke and Charles de Montesquieu. In these sources they found much support for their conviction that a key element for success in a democratic society is education. The education they envisioned was not a haphazard collection of current opinions, but a directed and purposeful endeavor intended to benefit both the individual and the nation, and to make political freedom possible.

No doubt the most significant education comes from the family, but in our system of government, the schools also play an important part. Ideas developed through education on all levels determine the outlook on the self, the family, society, as well as American democracy and citizenship. These thoughts establish the way we live politically, and also morally.

Morality has always been important in America because of our religious heritage and because of the way our Republic is designed to function. Of its nature, a democracy depends on the active involvement of its citizens. Without this it can hardly be called a democracy. And the people's participation depends on how they think about citizenship. This means consideration not only of their own behavior but also of the intellectual abilities and moral qualities of their representatives. Our Founders paid special attention to this because without citizens of good moral character who could recognize and elect representatives with the same characteristics, the nation could not survive as a free form of government. Inevitably, individual liberties would be lost, and anarchy or dictatorial rule would reappear, as had been the case with England's high-handed treatment of the colonies.

Noah Webster: On Knowledge and Freedom

One of the most vigorous proponents of general education in the revolutionary period was Noah Webster. As we have seen, his strong support for private property was one part of his recipe for the success of the new nation. The other part was his belief in the need for the general education of all citizens. One can easily understand the reason for this double requirement. The survival of the United States as a free republic depends on the rights of private property, coupled with sufficient understanding of its importance by the public. This is provided by education, which in turn makes intelligent voting possible. Webster believed that without moral training and possession of relevant facts, citizens could be misled by hucksters to approve dangerous policies that would benefit a few at the expense of everyone else. The best defense against this and other threats to basic freedoms was informed public instruction. He saw that infringements, although sometimes overt, are more often subtle and underhanded. Equipped with relevant knowledge, however, citizens could prevent their rights from gradually slipping away under the guise of short-term benefits bestowed by government or other parties.

"Information is fatal to despotism," said Webster. Much of his life was devoted to improving general education in this country by writing textbooks for use in schools and homes. He traveled throughout the States promoting them and was hugely successful. His spelling, grammar and reading books were used in American schools for over 100 years. These books, together with his dictionary, are the reason he has been called the "Father" of American education.

Among other things, Webster had strong feelings about language and history. He saw that the current emphasis on British forms of pronunciation, spelling and word definitions, and on European history, was not adequate for a new nation trying to find its own way. Added to that was the confusing assortment of dialects and foreign languages in use in this country. He found the pronunciation of words taught in schools "wretched," and wanted to remove "those distinctions of provincial dialects that are objects of reciprocal ridicule in the United States." To counteract the situation, he became a tireless worker for the development of an "American" language and history. He and other Founders believed that for the sake of national unity, they needed to promote the use of a single language throughout all States and encourage respect for the country by teaching American history and moral values ("Noah Webster," *Amherst College Library Exhibit*).

To deal with these problems, Webster wrote his *Grammatical Institute*, a three-part textbook that taught vocabulary, spelling, pronunciation, rules of grammar and reading skills. He strongly believed that all these things were needed to advance the cause of American citizenship and to overcome the alienation experienced by immigrants of so many different tongues and backgrounds. Webster's approach provided uniform spelling and pronunciation of English words in an American style. One of his innovations, the Spelling Bee, still survives. Instructions were accompanied by moral and patriotic lessons relevant to the American way of life.

The spelling book, the first part of his *Institute*, was often called "The Blue-backed Speller." It gave each word's spelling, pronunciation and meaning, as well as lessons in arithmetic, weights and measures and money values. Another important feature was a series of tales and aphorisms with moral lessons from the Bible, Aristotle, Aesop, Zeno and others. Intertwined with the subject matter the youngsters read sayings such as these (paraphrased):

> *Zeno taught that man has two ears and one tongue. This means that he should hear much and speak little.*

Hard labor is not good, but moderate labor is because it provides health, wealth and virtue.

The creation story teaches that God is great, and that he sees men's conduct.

The second part of the *Grammatical Institute* taught grammar, and the third part was titled, "An American Selection of Lessons in Reading and Speaking." Webster said that this section was necessary because the existing reading books, although competent for the most part, dealt mainly with European writings and subject matter. Webster's contribution was to present histories and materials of interest to Americans. There was a wide range of subjects covered, including a lengthy account of the life of Columbus, the history of the American Revolution, a number of dramas, conversations, orations and moral teachings. All of these readings were intended to improve the mind and help develop the character of America's young citizens.

In addition to these and many other writings, Webster created a monumental work called *An American Dictionary of the English Language*, which took twenty-seven years to complete. For this he traveled to Europe and studied twenty-six European, Asian and Near Eastern languages, including Hebrew, Latin and Greek, which he knew from his youth. His purpose was to discover the origins or etymologies of English words, which would help him produce a competent American version of the English language. He also wanted to provide appropriate political and moral interpretations.

This and his *Grammatical Institute* underwent many revisions and editions as he made corrections and adaptations to a living and changing language. His efforts established a foundation for American speech and writing that greatly improved communication skills among citizens, and at the same time helped develop a sense of national cohesion and pride in American culture.

His books obviously taught more than words. They gave context to the terms by referencing the Bible, moral teachings and American historical events. Students learned not only how to read and write, but also about their role in the American democratic experiment. For Webster and other Founders, the task of education was to provide the basic tools of knowledge, i.e., reading, writing, arithmetic and science, and also to put learning in the context of the rights and duties of citizenship. American republicanism required more than skills training. It was designed for a responsible citizenry, which includes both the knowledge and practice of ethical principles. The principles they had in mind were based on Christian moral values, which taught respect for the individual and the virtues of honesty, integrity and courage, to name a few. Webster wrote:

> In my view, the Christian religion is the most important and one of the first things in which all children, under a free government, ought to be instructed. The Christian religion must be the basis of any government intended to secure the rights and privileges of a free people.
> ("Noah Webster." Acton Institute)

In an essay on education, he wrote of the importance of teaching American history and of practical disciplines that enhance economic and social usefulness. Every small district should have a school, he wrote, taught by the most responsible and well-educated man there. Students should be taught the usual subjects, including the principles of liberty and government, which inculcate the principles of virtue and good behavior.

> The virtues of men are of more consequence to society than their abilities, and for this reason, the heart should be cultivated with more assiduity than the head.
> (*On the Education of Youth in America*)

"Virtue" had a range of meaning in those days, as it does today. Charles de Montesquieu, well known to the Founders, wrote that virtue was the bedrock of national survival. He gave it patriotic meaning, i.e., virtue was love of country. Webster felt this definition was too narrow and would not alone protect a nation from decay. But "if by virtue, writers mean *pure morals,* we shall all agree that such virtue is the true, safe and permanent foundation of a republic." Even this would not save a nation without a government dedicated to protecting the rights of every citizen (*Oration,* 5).

The Founders generally agreed on the importance of religion, but had differing views on church tenets and their implementation. Some wanted state-sanctioned churches, but others, led by Jefferson and Madison, insisted on freedom of worship and of opinion. In doing that they did not disparage religion or its importance in American life, as is thought by some people today. Their arguments over religion were generally parochial in nature, and concerned with coercive government-church interventions on individual rights. Basic biblical moral beliefs, however, were largely agreed-upon.

Today, as we witness the confusion, fear and cynicism that surround us, it is useful to recall our beginnings as a nation. During the war, the outcome of the Revolution was very uncertain, and following the victory new kinds of insecurity surfaced. The government was created in a period of turmoil, and it soon became clear that its success was not assured by the Constitution alone.

Webster captured the essence of the problem in a speech he gave on July 4th, 1802. His greatest concern, he said, was that during the past twenty-six years, many wartime civil and military leaders had passed away, and the new generation, which had not experienced the Revolution, may not realize the full extent of their predecessors' spirit and dedication to liberty. He feared the prospect of Americans becoming complacent, thinking that the new republican form of government would be sufficient to carry them through all difficulties.

After the experience of four or five thousand years, and the numberless forms of government, how should it happen to be reserved for the Americans to discover the great secret, which has eluded all former inquiry, of infusing into a political constitution, the quality of imperishable durability? (*Oration*, 2)

There are so many pitfalls to freedom that no form of government, of itself, could be expected to rescue Americans from tyranny. There is the danger of corruption of officials, the misunderstanding of individual liberties and property rights, the failure to create adequate and just voting procedures, the infighting between branches of government, and countless other hazards. Webster believed that republican government offered the best hope and that ours was an excellent example, but it would not stand for long without the constructive energy of the people. On July 4th, he enjoined his listeners to recall not only the glorious victory, but also the courage of those who fought and risked everything for freedom. It would be a crime to forget all those who lost their homes, their families and their own lives in the struggle. "So let the youth of our country…ponder the history and listen to the tale of their fathers' suffering, and their country's danger." He wanted them to learn of the deliberations of the first Congress, their goals, achievements and ideas of liberty. They should contemplate the character of these men and consider what is required of each generation to sustain freedom. It is that kind of knowledge that reveals the virtues of our forefathers and guards against corruptions of democratic principles. It offers the best assurance for America's future.

To encourage learning, Webster established schools and traveled throughout the States to promote learning relevant to the American scene. As noted, his *Grammatical Institute* was a great success. At one point he moved to Amherst, Connecticut, where he raised funds for a school and, as president of the board of trustees, opened Amherst Academy in 1815 to 90 girls and over 100 boys. The success of the Academy led to further fund-raising and the later founding of Amherst College for Christian ministry ("Noah Webster." Amherst College Library Exhibit).

Benjamin Rush: On Education and Religion

Webster's contemporary, Benjamin Rush, had similar thoughts and hopes for his country. The respect he gained as a medical doctor from Philadelphia no doubt helped him influence the revolutionary movement. After signing the Declaration of Independence and participating in the armed conflict, he later became a tireless advocate for a constitutional form of government. In his mind, the success of the new government depended on its form, to be sure, but even more on the preparation of its citizens to live in accord with it. On that subject Rush had strong views. The Constitution created special duties for every American, and these duties had to be learned. It was the task of the schools to inform young people of these requirements so that a coherent public social understanding could be formed (*A Defence of the Use of the Bible*). This was especially needed, he thought, in Pennsylvania because of the many different cultures of the immigrants there. He wanted a consistent form of education that would bring disparate peoples together as Americans rather than as loyalists to their native countries.

What should be the basis of this new type of education? "I beg leave to remark," he said, "that the only foundation for a useful education in a republic is to be laid in Religion. Without this there can be no virtue, and without virtue there can be no liberty, and liberty is the object and life of all republican governments." Rush believed this was so important that he would rather have the opinions of almost any religion taught than to have students grow up with no religious principles at all. However, the religion he recommended for this republic was that of the New Testament.

A Christian … cannot fail of being a republican, for every precept of the Gospel inculcates those degrees of humility, self-denial, and brotherly kindness, which are directly opposed to the pride of monarchy and the pageantry of a court. A Christian cannot fail of being useful to the republic, for his religion teacheth him, that no man "liveth to himself."

And lastly… his religion teacheth him, in all things to do to others what he would wish, in like circumstances, they should do to him. (*Of the Mode of Education*)

He wanted all schools to teach the history and principles of the American Revolution. Beyond that, the colleges should also have a series of courses on the history of ancient republics and of European governments. Learning of their successes and failures could be of great value in understanding the needs and possibilities of the new American society. The history and current state of commerce and money should also be taught, not only in the public schools but also in the seminaries. Knowledge of this kind, he said, is the best protection against hereditary monopolies and aristocracies. "I consider its effects as next to those of religion in humanizing mankind."

He also wanted the education of women, who were usually trained separately. He helped incorporate the Young Ladies Academy in Philadelphia to help them learn the same principles of liberty and government that the men learned. This was important, he said, because women are the first teachers of children and are essential supports for the men. They must not be excluded from the process of republican education (*Of the Mode of Education*).

Rush, Webster, Franklin and Jefferson all founded, or helped found, colleges to promote American-style education. They survive today as Dickinson College (1773), Amherst College (1821), The University of Pennsylvania (1749) and The University of Virginia (1819). Others contributed time and money to schools as well. Washington, for example, helped create what became Washington and Lee University and George Washington University, and Alexander Hamilton helped found Hamilton College.

Benjamin Franklin: On Support for Useful Education

As a youth, Franklin was poor, with little formal education. He worked hard and in time became self-sufficient and well-read. In later years he strongly promoted general education for the benefit of his state and the country. In 1749 he wrote a pamphlet entitled *Proposals Relating to the Education of Youth in Pensilvania* to gather funds and support for the Academy of Philadelphia, later known as the University of Pennsylvania. In his pamphlet he outlined the elements of useful education that he hoped would be incorporated in the curriculum. He cited Milton, Locke and other notables as references for his ideas. The right kind of education, he believed, would be of great value to individuals, the locality and the nation as a whole.

> The good Education of Youth has been esteemed by wise men of all Ages, as the surest Foundation of the Happiness both of private Families and of Commonwealths....
>
> Many of the first Settlers of these Provinces, were Men who had received a good Education in Europe, and to their Wisdom and good Management we owe much of our present Prosperity.

To continue their wise efforts, Franklin proposed a school, founded by men of means and "publick Spirit." It would be headed by a Rector, a man of good morals, with knowledge of languages and sciences. Franklin's curriculum would include arithmetic, geometry, English grammar, reading, pronunciation and several studies under the heading of history. History would teach ancient Greek and Roman events, geography, chronology, customs and the benefits of morality. It would show the necessity of public religion and the "Excellence of the CHRISTIAN RELIGION above all others antient or modern." Natural history, the history of commerce and mechanics would be combined with practical, hands-on gardening and farming arts.

He ended his essay with this:

> The Idea of what is *true Merit*, should also be often presented to Youth, explain'd and impress'd on their Minds, as consisting of an *inclination* join'd with an *Ability* to serve Mankind, one's Country, Friends and Family, which *Ability* is (with the Blessing of God) to be acquir'd or greatly encreas'd by *true Learning*; and should indeed be the great *Aim* and *End* of all Learning.

Franklin was hard to deal with at times and had his own ethical issues, but he recognized that good moral education was essential in the republic. He also showed considerable generosity toward those he thought would benefit from it productively.

Franklin was a poor man who made good. He strongly believed in the self-made man and tried to promote the virtues of hard work and social responsibility. In his will he stated that, unlike other Founders, he struggled as a youth but was supported by people who helped him get established. He never forgot that. His will created a trust to help "in forming and advancing other young men that may be serviceable to their country" (Isaacson, 474). In Boston the trust fund was used and grew as Franklin wished until, after 200 years, it was distributed to the B. Franklin Institute of Technology, then worth $5 million. In Philadelphia, the fund grew to only $2.3 million. Trustees said this was because money was distributed to poorer people who had more difficulty repaying. In any event, the trust illustrates Franklin's commitment to young citizens' efforts to become free and useful members of society.

George Washington: On Learning
and National Prosperity

Washington strongly believed in education, although he had only limited formal schooling himself. By age 15, he had learned the 3 R's and a few other subjects, including surveying, which became his early occupation. From then on he was self-educated. He read much, and in time amassed a large library. As President he tried repeatedly to promote education for the citizenry. In his Address to Congress in 1790, and in his Annual Address in 1796, he spoke of the importance of schools and proposed building a national university. That same year he gave $20,000 for a school in Virginia called Liberty Hall Academy, which later became Washington & Lee University. In 1821 he donated land near the White House for Columbian College, now George Washington University. In his will he gave $25,000 to promote a national university.

In his First Annual Message to Congress, he told the lawmakers:

> Nothing can better deserve your patronage than the promotion of Science and Literature...To the security of a free Constitution it contributes in various ways: By convincing [officials] that every valuable end of Government is best answered by the enlightened confidence of the people; and by teaching the people themselves to know and to value their own rights;... to distinguish between oppression and the necessary exercise of lawful authority;...to discriminate the spirit of Liberty from that of licentiousness...and uniting a speedy, but temperate vigilance against encroachments, with an inviolable respect to the Laws.

Like many others of his time, he saw the importance of schools for productive citizenship. Americans needed instruction in science, literature and history, and also in moral training. It should be noted that this moral training was not something separate from religion, but rather an integral part of it. Washington's view on this was typical of the times, and he was personally religious himself. He was often found praying alone in secluded spots, and publicly in his Episcopalian church, where he was a vestryman, and in public government buildings. When he disbanded the Army in 1783, he wrote a prayer to the Governors of the States: "I now make it my earnest prayer that God would have you, and the State over which you preside, in his holy protection; …that he would … dispose us all to do justice, to love mercy, and to demean ourselves with that charity, humility, and pacific temper of mind, which were the characteristics of the Divine Author of our blessed religion."

He lived as a Christian, although he seems to have had difficulty with some church practices and doctrines. At any rate, his detractors called him a Deist, whatever that was supposed to mean. That charge is still heard, although in a different context. Then, the term was used pejoratively, but had little meaning beyond the fact that he and several other Founders were not as "orthodox" as some thought they should be.

One example of "unorthodox" behavior was his 1775 order to the troops forbidding them to burn the Pope in effigy on Guy Fawkes Night. Another was a letter Washington wrote to Jewish leaders in 1790 that said he wanted a country: "which gives to bigotry no sanction, to persecution no assistance…May the Children of the Stock of Abraham, who dwell in this land, continue to merit and enjoy the good will of the other inhabitants; while every one shall sit under his own vine and fig tree, and there shall be none to make him afraid" ("George Washington").

Washington made mistakes and acknowledged many of them, but he was also a man dedicated to prayer and the promotion of Christian moral values. A fine example of his thinking is found in his Farewell Address when leaving the office of President:

> Of all the dispositions and habits, which lead to political prosperity, Religion and Morality are indispensable supports.
>
> In vain would that man claim the tribute of Patriotism, who should labor to subvert these great pillars of human happiness, these firmest props of the duties of Men and Citizens… And let us with caution indulge the supposition that morality can be maintained without

religion. Whatever may be conceded to the influence of refined education on minds of peculiar structure, reason and experience both forbid us to expect that national morality can prevail in exclusion of religious principle.

John Adams: On Knowledge, Virtue and Religion

Another strong advocate of American education was John Adams. Like others of his time, he believed that the structure of the new government required promulgation of basic knowledge to help people understand their rights and duties as republican citizens. There were economic and political reasons for this, and they both depended on the knowledge and practice of moral principles. It was not assumed that people would instinctively know how to live in a democratic republic without suitable instruction in these areas. In fact, he believed that the future of the nation depended on it.

Before the U.S. Constitution was formed, Adams was the principal writer of one for the Commonwealth of Massachusetts. It is today the oldest constitution in the world still in use. It played a large role in the formulation of the U.S Constitution, which was patterned after it in many respects.

Massachusetts had appointed John and Samuel Adams, together with James Bowdoin, to draft a constitution, but the work of writing it fell to John. It was finished and agreed upon by the Delegates in 1780. Article I states the unalienable right to life and liberty, and that of acquiring and protecting property. Article II outlines the rights and duties of citizens to worship God and to learn and follow religious moral precepts. For this, support for teachers of public religious and moral instruction was needed. The form of worship and instruction was to be Christian, but every man retained the right to form his own opinion and to live according to his conscience. No religious denomination was to be preferred to any other, and none could ever be established by law.

Adams' notion of education revolved around these points. Well educated himself, he understood the value of learning in the sciences, literature and especially history and religion. Men can "plan and speculate for Liberty, but it is Religion and Morality alone, which can establish the Principles upon which Freedom can securely stand." In his Inaugural Address as President, he spoke of his

> love of science and letters, and a wish to patronize every rational effort to encourage schools, colleges, universities, academies, and every institution for propagating knowledge, virtue, and religion among all classes of the people, not only for their benign influence on the happiness of life, in all its stages and classes, and of society in all its forms, but as the only means of preserving our constitution from all its natural enemies …

In that same speech he expressed his veneration for the Christian religion, and observed that he considered "a decent respect for Christianity among the best recommendations for the public service."

Thomas Jefferson: On Education
and Freedom of Conscience

His successor, Jefferson, was not as enthusiastic about public religious education as Washington and Adams were, but this was because of his fear of state-sanctioned churches. Several colonies had government-authorized churches that demanded compliance with their beliefs and practices, as well as taxes to support them. Jefferson was strongly opposed to this, based on his belief in freedom of conscience. Although his understanding of freedom of conscience is a traditional Christian belief, he was denounced as an atheist, deist and hater of religion. But a look at his life reveals something else. He was a student of the Bible, participated in public days of prayer, regularly attended church services, including those given in the U.S. Capitol and other public buildings, married in the church, sent his children to a Christian school, contributed to religious congregations and encouraged Christian missions to the Indians. He supported legislation that put chaplains on the public payroll and provided money for a priest's salary and church for the Indians. He also wrote an abridged version of the New Testament in four languages which focused on the moral teachings of Jesus.

He knew the moral value of religion for America and for himself, and he regarded Jesus as the greatest moral teacher who ever lived. But because he did not accept certain dogmas of the church, and especially because he insisted on freedom of conscience and expression for every individual, he was accused of being an enemy of religion. His campaign for freedom of religion did have supporters, however, and their efforts resulted in the Constitution's First Amendment prohibition of government-established churches. On the state level, his own direct efforts were instrumental in creating Virginia's law on religious tolerance, which he considered one of his most important contributions.

That achievement was noted on his tombstone. He wrote the act in 1779, shortly after the Declaration of Independence, although it was not adopted until 1786 under the title, *The Virginia Act For Establishing Religious Freedom*. It is a precise statement of his simultaneous respect for religion coupled with his disdain for coercive measures to support particular churches.

> Well aware that Almighty God hath created the mind free; that all attempts to influence it by temporal punishments or burdens, or by civil incapacitations... are a departure from the plan of the Holy Author of our religion...; that the impious presumption of legislators and rulers, civil as well as ecclesiastical... who have assumed dominion over the faith of others, setting up their own opinions and modes of thinking as the only true and infallible, and as such endeavoring to impose them on others...; that to

compel a man to furnish contributions of money for the propagation of opinions which he disbelieves, is sinful and tyrannical…Be it therefore enacted by the General Assembly, that no man shall be compelled to frequent or support any religious worship, place or ministry whatsoever…; but that all men shall be free to profess, and by argument to maintain, their opinions in matters of religion…

Jefferson wanted freedom of conscience to be cultivated in terms of Christian moral understanding, but while morals should be taught and encouraged, they should not be forced on anyone. Like other Founders, he regarded general education as essential for the health of the nation. He proposed a school system for Virginia that provided for the education of every child for at least three years, and longer for the better students. It was free for those parents who could not afford it. The first stage focused on basic skills of reading, writing and arithmetic for all children and then, for the more gifted students, Greek, Latin, geography and mathematics in grammar schools. The best of these would go on to William and Mary College to study the sciences and disciplines suitable to their individual abilities. European and American history was essential throughout because all Americans needed to understand the background that led to the formation of the American government. Also, moral instruction was necessary to orient students toward productive and happy lives as citizens.

Later in life, he designed and founded the University of Virginia, one of his proudest accomplishments. His thoughts on religious education were expressed in the curriculum. No regular faculty member taught religion, but space was provided on campus for each church to teach its own particular theology. In that way, conflicts between religious bodies vying for representation in the standard curriculum could be avoided, while students could have the religious instruction that was in accord with their own interests and beliefs.

Jefferson was a fervent believer in the value of human reason, but not uninformed reason. In his view: "If a nation expects to be ignorant and free in a state of civilization, it expects what never was and never will be." People needed to be taught information and methods of dealing with it in order to make wise decisions. American freedom depended on basic education of the masses as well as advanced schooling for those capable of it. To Madison he wrote: "I hope the education of the common people will be attended to, convinced that on their good sense we may rely with the most security for the preservation of a due degree of liberty" (Coates).

James Madison: On Democratic Education

Jefferson and his good friend, James Madison, viewed education almost in the same light. Both regarded general education a must for the nation, and both opposed forced religious participation in schools or anywhere else. Madison promoted general education in the States, as did others, since the Constitution did not provide for national schools. His views are summarized in a letter he wrote to W.T. Barry in 1822 praising the legislature of Kentucky for making sizeable appropriations for general education.

> A popular Government, without popular information, or no means of acquiring it, is but a Prologue to a Farce or a Tragedy; or, perhaps both. Knowledge will forever govern ignorance: And a people who mean to be their own Governors must arm themselves with the power that knowledge gives.

Madison pointed out the error of those who think of education only in terms of colleges and universities for the wealthy, as if no one else has an interest in learning. If the rich educate only themselves, the whole society suffers. Unlike a monarchy or aristocracy, a democratic form of government demands a much broader interest in education. Educating many rather than a few makes rule by the people possible. He thought America needed higher education for advanced learning in science, literature, history and other disciplines for economic and political success, and also for preparation of teachers. It is the learned institutions that are "the nurseries of skilful Teachers for the schools distributed throughout the Community." This is how knowledge is best distributed throughout society, and how the individual talents of the most people are discovered. With this approach, students, regardless of class, have an opportunity to learn and contribute to the state and nation.

Madison viewed education in terms of his encompassing view of property. He made clear that property was more than land, money and tangible possessions. It also includes the personal strengths and qualities of the individual. John Locke had said, "...every man has a property in his own person. This nobody has any right to but himself." His property is his "life, liberty and estate," and the product of his labor belongs to him alone. Madison laid special emphasis on this notion. Property is all that belongs to each person. It comprises not only land and the fruit of one's labor in tangible external goods, but one's thoughts and moral convictions as well. Labor produces goods and revenue based on thoughts and ideas, and ideas are learned through education. This concept of property requires the education of the person, which in turn makes freedom possible. The more people who understand this, he believed, the happier the entire society will be. "What spectacle can be more edifying or more seasonable, than that of Liberty and Learning, each leaning on the other for their mutual and surest support?"

Madison and other Founders were indebted in a number of ways to Enlightenment thinkers like Charles de Montesquieu. Montesquieu's ideas on the republican form of government and the separation of powers are reflected in our Constitution. As part of this type of government, he stressed the importance of public virtue. Of the three basic forms of government – monarchical, republican and despotic – two rely principally on the dictates of one or a few rulers, with the populous simply following along.

In republican governments, men are all equal. Equal they are also in despotic governments: in the former because they are everything; in the latter, because they are nothing.

(*Spirit of Laws*, Book 6)

Of the three, only the republican requires that citizens be virtuous, since they are the responsible authorities themselves. Kings and despots can rule on their own terms, but without public virtue, republican society cannot succeed (*Spirit of Laws*, Book. 8).

John Locke was another who believed that public virtue in a republic was essential, and wrote at length on the connection between that and education. But whereas Montesquieu's virtue, according to Webster, was largely patriotic in nature, Locke discussed virtue as personal development and strength. The very foundation of education had to be rooted in moral education.

I place *virtue* as the first and most necessary of those endowments that belong to a man or a gentleman, as absolutely requisite to make him valued and beloved by others, acceptable or tolerable to himself. Without that, I think, he will be happy neither in this nor the other world.

As a foundation of this, there ought very early to be imprinted on his mind a true notion of *God*...Maker of all things, from whom we receive all our goods, who loves us and gives us all things....

These are my present thoughts concerning learning and accomplishments. The great business of all is *virtue* and *wisdom*. [It is vital to teach the student] to get a mastery over his inclinations and *submit his appetite to reason*. This being obtained, and by constant practice settled into habit, the hardest part of the task is over…(*Thoughts Concerning Education*, 102-03; 152)

Locke thought that education becomes effective when the student acquires virtue through discipline (firm but not harsh) and the Christian belief in God. Biblical and moral instruction was needed, and he had special regard for the study of theology, provided it was not corrupted by partisan interests (*Conduct of the Understanding*, 195).

Madison followed this line of reasoning, but made an exceptionally strong appeal for freedom of conscience. His views on the curriculum were similar to most of his contemporaries, except for religious education, where he echoed Jefferson. In fact, Madison may have held even stronger views on religious separation than Jefferson. It is said that he was influenced as a youth by seeing some Baptist ministers jailed for preaching in an Anglican district. This probably was a factor in his desire to keep governments from instituting official churches and creating laws that demand compliance with specific teachings and practices. Especially galling to him was forced payment of church taxes. No doubt another factor was the influence of his early Scottish tutors, and later of professors at the College of New Jersey (Princeton), who exemplified the spirit of American resistance to coercive authority.

In 1785 Madison wrote *Memorial and Remonstrance Against Religious Assessments* in which he objected to a bill being debated in Virginia's Assembly. The bill, supported by Patrick Henry, George Washington, George Mason and others, would establish legal support for teachers of Christianity. No specific church was named, and those who objected could assign their required tax support to other educational causes. Still, Madison protested. Religion, he wrote in his *Remonstrance*, is based on reason and conscience, and cannot be subject to the authority of any legislative body:

Who does not see that the same authority which can establish Christianity, in exclusion of all other Religions, may establish with the same ease any particular sect of

Christians, in exclusion of all other Sects?... Whilst we assert for ourselves a freedom to embrace, to profess and to observe the Religion which we believe to be of divine origin, we cannot deny an equal freedom to those whose minds have not yet yielded to the evidence which has convinced us. If this freedom be abused, it is an offense against God, not against man.

His Religious Assessments bill failed, and in its place Jefferson's bill establishing religious freedom, cited earlier, was enacted.

Today we may underestimate the strength of the desire for church-affiliated laws in early America. Even after the Bill of Rights was enacted, attempts were made to create government churches. Jefferson saw it during his administration, and Madison actually vetoed a bill sent to him by Congress in 1811 that would have established the Episcopal Church as the official church of Alexandria in the District of Columbia. In doing so, he had to point out that the First Amendment specifically forbids the Congress from doing that.

We must not confuse the cautious attitudes of Jefferson and Madison on public church involvements with their private views on religion itself. Nor must we assume that their views on this were typical of their contemporaries. Today, we hear more about the ideas of these two men than of almost all other Founders on this topic. But their ideas were not in the majority, regardless of their merits, because of the urgency felt by many to ensure adequate moral training for the people at large. Webster, Rush, Washington, Adams and many others argued strongly for Bible reading and Christian teaching in public schools. But which Christian teaching? Should any one interpretation be preferred over the others? Jefferson and Madison provided a valuable service in dealing with these questions by checking the excesses of religious zealots, but they did not thereby deny religion's place in society or their own dedication to it.

CHAPTER 6

American Religion and the Spirit of Freedom: On Education

We profess to be republicans, and yet we neglect the only means of establishing and perpetuating our republican forms of government; that is, the universal education of our youth in the principles of Christianity by means of the Bible; for this divine book, above all others, favors that equality among mankind, that respect for just laws, and all those sober and frugal virtues which constitute the soul of republicanism.
(Benjamin Rush)

In the early days of the Republic, Bible reading was considered an important part of education, although there were heated arguments over which church interpretation was superior and which should be taught to the young. Some felt the way around these disagreements was simply to omit Bible teachings in the schools. But attempts to do this were strenuously opposed. Where would the citizens find this knowledge if not in the schools, where people typically learned to read the Bible? How would people discover the biblical moral teachings needed in democratic society? Benjamin Rush was one of many who strongly believed in the value of Bible reading in the schools for personal benefit and for the health of the nation. His efforts made him a leader among the Founders in the belief that republicanism depended on moral knowledge, the best of which was found in the Bible.

Many studies have been done on European influences on American political thought, such as Enlightenment philosophy and earlier Greek and Roman ideas that come to us through European sources. Less is known about the influence of the Bible on these sources and on early Americans. It is important to recognize this because the mindset of our Founders was grounded in biblical teaching, which in turn helped them form their notions of government and the possibilities of self-government. This becomes clearer if we are able to separate the lively debates of the time over particular religious doctrines from the consensus that existed on biblical moral principles.

The Founders' interest in education is consistent with their upbringing in a religious culture. They understood, as did their forebears for thousands of years, that human beings are not automatically programmed for successful living. People learn some things from personal experience, but much more from the example and teachings of others. They are not like other animals that rely more heavily on basic instincts to survive. Knowledge of the Bible is especially useful for this purpose because it records the history of human experiences and teachings that span thousands of years. It extends the human drama far beyond the parameters of European history and philosophy to ancient sources that became the foundation of the western world. That perspective is reflected in the Founders' thinking on human strengths and failings, and on the type of government best suited for Americans. It explains their insistence on quality general education, which enables the system to work.

It would be hard to separate early American views on political life from the Judeo-Christian heritage (D'Souza, 5). The Bible provided stories of a vast array of human experiences over many centuries in many different historical situations. The lesson, repeated over and over, is that to live well, people must live by the guidelines and laws of God. It was promulgated by inspired teachers and passed on to subsequent generations by their disciples and their disciples after them. It survived the test of time, although it came close to dying out on more than one occasion.

The importance of religious instruction is highlighted in the figures of Moses and Jesus, both of whom spent inordinate amounts of time teaching. The prophets, wise men and other teachers who followed were dedicated to keeping the message alive. The whole Book is a collection of teachings, and it was through these instructions that many subsequent generations developed their orientation and sense of purpose in life. Knowledge of biblical ideas fostered the Founders' conviction that, despite human frailties, which the Bible fully exposed and also were known through their personal experiences, Americans had the potential and character for self-government. They saw that intelligent teaching was indispensable, because it enables people to quickly acquire useful knowledge that would take generations to learn solely by personal experience.

THE BIBLE

Ancient Constitutions: The Covenants

When our Founders conceived of the idea of a national constitution, they had many precedents to draw from. History provided useful examples from Greece, Rome and later European nations which helped them establish a political framework. But underlying that was a biblical perspective known to these nation builders through their religious studies and practices. It is important to recognize this because the biblical lessons that influenced them are not as well-known today as they were then.

The Bible has always been read for personal religious reasons, but there is also a wealth of historical information about the rise and fall of communities and nations that is useful to anyone who values historical knowledge. One age-old lesson continually stressed in the Bible is the importance of honoring valid contracts.

In many ways and in many different circumstances, the Bible records public agreements that provided direction and purpose for the community. These were business contracts, national treaties, marriages, labor arrangements and ritual requirements, all having legal connotations and all under the auspices of religion. Religion, the bond between God and the people, was not a separate part of life, as it is conceived today. It included the agreements just listed as well as the customs of the society. In Israel, life revolved around these rules or covenants, with the Mosaic Law having the weight of what we might call the national constitution. Israel's successes and failures were measured in terms of covenantal compliance or rejection. Our Founders knew this history and its challenges well, and it played an important role in their vision of a viable constitutional society. A brief look at this history helps us better understand their perspective.

The Old Testament (The Hebrew Bible)

The greatest of the biblical agreements recorded in the Old Testament is the Sinai Covenant. After Moses received the Law at Mt. Sinai, and the people accepted it, he spent the rest of his life teaching and exhorting his people to follow it. The Covenant was structured in some ways like the ancient Code of Hammurabi, and especially like a Hittite suzerainty treaty, known at that time as an agreement between a king or suzerain and his subjects. The Hittite king offered protection, and his people promised loyalty to the provisions of the covenant (Mendenhall, 26-46). These were legal contracts that formed what we today could call constitutions. In Israel's case the Sinai Covenant became the basis of its political, as well as its religious life. Its impact has been felt ever since. The Pilgrims no doubt had it in mind when they wrote their Mayflower Compact (*Interpreter's Bible*, 992). Other colonies and states also drew on this precedent.

The history of Israel is a story of successes and failures to abide by covenant guidelines. Bad will was a constant problem, but another was failure to even know what the Law taught. Prophets, ministers, wisdom teachers and others arose again and again to remind the people of their Covenant and to instruct them in its requirements. Each generation needed to learn anew the message Moses had given, and when that did not happen, the people drifted into aimless and harmful pursuits. Our Founders foresaw this risk, which is why they believed the future of the constitutional form of government they formed was dependent on meaningful education.

The Wisdom Teachers

When Solomon became king, he brought into his court wise men to instruct the young. Several books of the Bible reflect this tradition. In them are found practical bits of advice for daily living (proverbs) and reflections on the meaning and purpose of life. Some psalms belong to this tradition, as do Job, Proverbs, Sirach, Wisdom and other books. It is a different style of teaching than Moses the lawgiver used, but it belongs to the same worldview. It is intensely concerned with education. Much of it exhorts students to embrace "discipline," i.e., guidelines and instructions on how to live daily life.

Early Americans were attuned to this concept of discipline because they realized, by teaching and experience, that survival depended on self-restraint and focused attention on the business of life. Prosperity came forth from careful observation of events, hard work and the requirements of justice. The Bible contains many useful lessons on these subjects.

The wisdom teachings exhort listeners to accept instruction and conform their lives to the dictates of wisdom. In Proverbs, Wisdom speaks:

To you, O men, I call; my appeal is to the children of men.

You simple ones, gain resource, you fools, gain sense…

[When God created the world] I [was] beside him as his craftsman, and I was his delight day by day, playing before him all the while, playing on the surface of his earth; and I found delight in the sons of men.

So now, O children, listen to me; instruction and wisdom do not reject! Happy the man who obeys me, and happy those who keep my ways… For he who finds me finds life, and wins favor from the Lord; But he who misses me harms himself; all who hate me love death. (Proverbs 8:4f.)

The book of Proverbs contains this poetic style of wisdom teaching, but it also gives very down-to-earth practical advice: "Ill-gotten treasures profit nothing, but virtue saves from death….A wise man heeds commands, but a prating fool will be overthrown….He who winks at a fault causes trouble, but he who frankly reproves promotes peace" (Proverbs 10). Solomon and his court recognized the value of this kind of discipline for the young and especially for their leaders.

The key to Israel's survival was not economic or military strength; it was moral rectitude, measured by biblical teachings. Colonial Americans used similar guidelines to encourage personal moral strengths, which in turn created awareness of the possibility of independence based on the rule of the people.

The Prophets

After Solomon, the kingdom was split into two parts because of dissension between the tribes. During that time Israel produced a long line of reformers. Among them were the biblical prophets, who followed in the footsteps of Moses by pointing out in strong terms the failures of the people and the need to return to the Covenant. The eighth century prophets Amos and Hosea roundly condemned the immoral practices of the kings and their subjects in the Northern Kingdom. The result of their infidelity, they said, would be the destruction of the nation, and so it happened. Later, in the Southern Kingdom, Isaiah, Jeremiah, Micah and others taught the same message.

Religion was usually thought of in ritualistic terms. It concerned sacrificial ceremonies led by priests who offered worship in sanctuaries and the Temple to gain favor with God. The prophets implored the people to think bigger: ritual worship was meaningless unless accompanied by justice and love. The priests and leaders of society had failed by not teaching that this was true knowledge of God:

> The Lord has a grievance against the inhabitants of the land:
>
> There is no fidelity, no mercy, no knowledge of God. False swearing, lying, murder, stealing and adultery! In their lawlessness bloodshed follows bloodshed. Therefore the land mourns, and everything that dwells in it languishes....
>
> For it is love that I desire, not sacrifice, and knowledge of God rather than holocausts. (Hosea 4:1-3; 6:6)

The prophets were the greatest teachers of their time, trying to direct the people's attention to the spirit of the Law, but for the most part they were ignored. Most Israelites hardly noticed that they had lapsed into customs that were destroying the society. The greatest sin was idolatry, which involved far more than worship of statues. The religions of Baal, Molech, Asherah, Topheth, Chemosh and other pagan gods practically obliterated the moral codes of Israel. Among these pagan practices were fertility rites of drunkenness and orgies, witchcrafts and human sacrifices. Little children were immolated to worship Molech and other gods. Unwise foreign treaties were made. Cheating, bribery, stealing and other injustices oppressed the poor and drove many into slave-like conditions. All these things were condemned by the Law, and despite the warnings of the prophets, the nation of Israel disintegrated and was eventually destroyed, first by Assyria and then by Babylonia.

It was clear to later generations that the prophets had seen the disaster coming and had made the right call. Our Founders were well aware of this insight and tried to create a political climate that would avoid political collapse by stressing the importance of education. The circumstances were different from ancient times but the lesson was the same. The only question was whether or not each generation of Americans could learn it. It is the same question we ask today.

The Kings

Israel produced a number of outstanding teachers, but there were too few of them and they were often misunderstood. The people simply had wandered too far from their Mosaic heritage. Kings often led the way to depravity, which is what the Founders thought George III was doing, but there were a few Israelite kings who made efforts to awaken the people to their original faith. They did this by destroying pagan shrines and by proclaiming feasts and rituals to honor Yahweh. Some were especially dedicated to teaching the Mosaic Law. Jehoshaphat, for example, sent fifteen of his leading men to every town in Judah with the book of the Law to instruct the people (2 Chronicles 17).

Unless such efforts were ongoing, however, Israel would forget and slide back into self-serving and immoral practices. By the time of Hezekiah, the temple worship in Jerusalem was defunct. He realized this and worked to restore the rundown temple and reestablish Judaic religion throughout his kingdom. For this he had the help of important teachers and prophets like Isaiah and Micah. But by the time his great-grandson, Josiah, became king, his reform had been almost completely forgotten. Josiah, seeing that the temple of Solomon had been neglected, ordered a restoration. During the restoration, Moses' book of the Law was discovered in the temple. No one of that generation had ever read it or knew what it said. Josiah was shocked by its contents and had it read publicly in its entirety. It showed the people how far they had strayed, and caused Josiah to eliminate all pagan shrines and practices in the land. Among them were foreign religious objects and rites in the temple itself. There were even apartments for fertility-cult prostitutes there, which Josiah destroyed (2 Kings 23). At the time, apparently no one realized that these cults were forbidden by the Law. They probably seemed acceptable because of the proximity and familiarity of Canaanite religions, and also because Solomon and later kings married foreign women who brought their religions with them into Israel. These non-Israelite conventions could be called "education" of a sort, but it was the wrong kind.

The Bible leaves nothing unsaid about the failures of Israel, but it is not nihilistic. Its writings were meant for the people of the time, as well as for future generations, and they did not convey hopeless despair. The point was not to give up hope but to learn from the mistakes of the past. In that respect they succeeded if one considers the fact that Abraham's people have been known to history for nearly four thousand years. It is hard to imagine that blood ties alone account for this. The monarchical period alone, from Saul to the Babylonian Exile, was twice as long as the time from George Washington to the present. Many tribes and nations that once thrived have disappeared from history, yet the Hebrew tradition still lives among Jews and Christians. Covenant faith must be an important reason that this is so.

Israel's story of the teaching role of the kings was relevant to America's early leaders. As President, Washington promoted the education of citizens' political rights and responsibilities, and publicly prayed and taught the value of religion, as did his successors. It was considered a responsibility of leadership to encourage the people to know and live by the spirit of their Constitution with its political/religious/moral underpinnings.

The Scribes

The Bible attributes Israel's demise to its failure to practice its authentic religion. After the Babylonian Exile, Ezra the scribe made it his life's work to restore Israel to the teachings of the Law or Torah. Knowledge of the Law, he taught, was the key to survival and prosperity. Today, the histories of nations are described mainly in political, economic and military terms, but the Bible sees those factors as results rather than causes of national events. Israel had failed before because of the people's ignorance and rebellion against the Law, but now, after learning the hard lessons of exile, there was hope that that a new age of prosperity would begin. The precepts of the Law were both liturgical and ethical, and if the people were successful at applying those precepts to their personal lives, their political/economic life would also be successful. Ezra's efforts united Mosaic codes with the wisdom literature by identifying the Law as the revelation of God's wisdom; it was through the Law, he said, that God's wisdom was revealed.

Ezra, like Jehoshaphat and Josiah, read the book of Moses to the people, who again, as in past times, were ignorant of it. To the assembly of the people, Ezra "read out of the book from daybreak to midday… and all the people listened attentively to the book of the law." Then, for seven days they celebrated the feast of Booths, described in the law, for seven days. "Ezra read from the book of the law of God day after day, from the first day to the last" (Nehemiah 9). Because of Ezra's efforts to reacquaint the people with their covenant, the returning exiles made a pact establishing the Mosaic Law as the constitution of their nation. From that time on Israel had scribes following Ezra's example of teaching the people the meaning of their covenant or constitution with God and one another. By the time of Jesus, however, legalistic and erroneous interpretations had crept in which Jesus condemned, often in the style of the pre-exilic prophets.

The Founders' Lesson

From the time of Moses, and even before that, education was the fundamental instrument that directed and unified national life. Brute force was in the picture too, especially under the kings, and there were numerous breakdowns in and among the tribes, but the main thing that held the people together was belief in their Covenant. In post-exilic times, with no kingdom and no king, the Torah became Israel's explicit constitution, unaccompanied by strong central government. Civil authority no longer had the force it had under the kings, so survival of the nation now depended almost exclusively on knowledge and observance of the Law. We may be sure that our Founders were aware of this history and saw its relevance to their new nation. They knew that their Constitution and its moral spirit would quickly whither unless each generation was taught its meaning. Complying with the letter of the law required little more than military and police force, as was the case under the monarchy, but for a people to be free they had to be able to live by the spirit of the law. It is the reason that John Adams, Benjamin Rush and so many others believed that their new government was fit only for an educated and moral people.

The New Testament

The Covenant-Constitution Connection

There is a connection between covenant and constitution that must have been more obvious to the Founders than it is today. Living in the religious culture of eighteenth century America, they knew that behind both legal structures is the element of trust or faith. For religion to be viable, people must believe their covenant is true and trust in God; in a democratic republic, people must believe their constitution deserves to be honored and trust in the citizens, who are themselves the leaders.

In ancient Israel, these two beliefs were combined in civil and religious organizations, as they often are in nations, but in America they are legally separated. This separation leads secularists to conclude that religion should play no part in political life. However, that is not how the Founders saw it. The separation they envisioned exists only up to a point. It prohibits government interference with religion, but not the exercise of religion. Religion cannot be forced on people by political means, but the trust that religion brings to society is invaluable in constitutional government. Trust underlies both religion and politics, and education is the catalyst that supports the stability of both.

Were They Rebels or Reformers?

The New Testament records the continuation of Israel's history of renewal. As before, this new reform was accepted by some, misunderstood by many and vehemently rejected by some religious and political authorities, who felt threatened. John the Baptist was beheaded, Jesus was crucified and many of his disciples were jailed, dispersed or killed. Yet the message survived. One of the reasons it did was that almost all of the earliest Christians were Jews and the new message, as revolutionary as it seemed to be, was not fundamentally alien to Judaism. There were new elements in it, with its heavy emphasis on Jesus' messianic role and its de-emphasis on legalistic practices, but originally it was mainly a call for a return to the true religion of Israel. The message of the prophets and great leaders of the past had faded in the distance, and the post-exilic reform of Ezra and his contemporaries had become excessively legalistic.

Jesus and his followers set out to bring the religion of Moses back to life and did so by means of preaching and teaching, as had been done in Israel so many times before. John the Baptist and Jesus called for the people to "Repent," which means "return" to the Covenant religion. What appeared to some to be radical comments and actions by Jesus on the Sabbath and other occasions addressed this need. They were wake-up calls, pointing to the excessively legalistic and ritualistic conditions of the time, and they served to infuriate religious authorities.

The New Testament called on people to accept Jesus and His message, which caused great turmoil among leaders of the Jews. Most thought of Him as a troublemaker and did not accept Him as Messiah, but a bigger concern may have been that the Gospel message was proclaimed publicly. As they and the Romans saw it, this preaching was stirring up the people to question the religious and political powers of authorities. Even though the Gospel was largely consistent with the spirit of Jewish tradition, leaders were severely threatened and resolved to silence its messengers.

There were echoes of this experience in early America. Authorities in England also felt threatened by reformist preaching and teaching. Samuel Adams was considered a traitor for publicly agitating for citizen's rights in Boston, but he soon had many followers. In both first and eighteenth century cases there were religious, political and economic elements involved, and both were struggles over freedom. In America there had been ongoing efforts to protect religious freedoms for some, but restrict them for others, and prior to the Revolution political and economic freedoms had been granted to some but denied others by Parliament and the King. The original intention of the protest against England was to restore the freedoms colonists had known earlier. Initially, colonists did not rebel by trying to create a new government. Instead, they were asking for citizens' rights already known in Europe, many of which had biblical precedents. But the authorities, who did have some legitimate concerns, rejected most of the colonists' petitions. England needed income to pay for wars, one of which was fought in America, and they objected to the supposed ingratitude of colonists who resisted taxation and government regulations.

The King continued to harden his position without success until he finally declared, "blows will decide." The violence that broke out split the people into two separate camps, and then into separate nations – but they did not separate completely. Just as early Christians retained much of Jewish tradition, the new nation relied on the best of European thought and culture to form the government and continued to do so long after the

Revolution. As mentioned earlier Locke, Montesquieu and others were formative influences. America created a new nation, but was heavily indebted to European religion and philosophy as it formed a pioneering governmental structure and grew into a viable political and economic phenomenon. This could not have been done without educated leaders with knowledge of western history and learning.

Another interesting relationship between the biblical and American experiences is found in the extraordinary bravery demonstrated by the reformers (See *Courage and the Revolutionary Spirit* on pages 53-55). Whatever faults we may find with the Founders, we must recognize the strength of their resolve and the sacrifices they made because of it. Today the inspiration drawn from their Christian faith is often underestimated. They knew the path Jesus and the martyrs had taken, and the price they had paid for following their convictions. Early Christians faced imprisonment and death for refusing to abandon their principles, and so did the American revolutionaries. The first century reformers may have sacrificed more for a longer time, but the Americans, in the same spirit, knowingly invited a great deal of trouble for themselves by revolting. They realized from the beginning that the stakes were high, but that freedom carried a high price.

They had this in common with the early Christians: they were able to persevere with great courage in the face of intense pressure by powerful authorities. The early Christians were almost totally non-violent, while Americans believed in self-defense, but both found inspiration in the biblical precedent of refusing to back down in the face of fierce opposition. It cost many of them severely, but made the freedom they sought possible for most of them and for a great many others over the years.

The Apostolic and American Teaching Missions

The New Testament movement had a strong educational component. Jesus taught daily in the synagogues, the Temple and in public places. So did Peter, together with other apostles, deacons and disciples. Paul taught for years in synagogues and publicly to anyone who would listen. The mission of all the Christians was to proclaim the Gospel and live its message by example. The oral message was comprised of preaching (<u>kerygma</u> – proclaiming the word) and teaching (<u>didache</u> – giving moral instruction) (Dodd). Listeners were attracted by the preaching of the Gospel, and those interested were given further instruction on the moral life that was expected of Christians. Originally oral, various versions of the message were later committed to written gospels. The New Testament contains the four most important of these.

A critical element in the survival and spread of Christianity was the teaching function of its members. Paul was a leading figure in the teaching role, traveling far and wide to instruct all who would listen. He was an intense believer in the principle, often underestimated, that the message first must be fully understood before it can be accepted and practiced authentically. Early Americans followed the same methodology.

Our Founders did not assume that their ideas and achievements would be fully understood, even in their own time, and then automatically passed along to later generations. They continually taught the virtues of republicanism publicly and encouraged families, churches and schools to do the same. The education provided had to be of high quality. As we saw earlier, Noah Webster put forth enormous efforts to promote this, as did others, and here again there was a biblical precedent.

The prophets and wise men of Israel were renowned for their wholehearted dedication to Covenant teaching, and this was due to their knowledge and moral strength. In the New Testament, the model for this is Jesus. He is called a prophet in the tradition of earlier prophets, and also a wisdom teacher. John introduced his gospel with a description of Jesus that brings to mind the Old Testament personification of Wisdom:

> In the beginning was the Word; the Word was in God's presence, and the Word was God. He was present to God in the beginning. Through him all things came into being…

Whatever came to be in him found life, life for the light of men. The light shines on in darkness, a darkness that did not overcome it....

The Word became flesh and made his dwelling among us, and we have seen his glory: the glory of an only Son coming from the Father, filled with enduring love...

For while the law was given through Moses, this enduring love came through Jesus Christ. No one has ever seen God.

It is God the only Son, ever at the Father's side, who has revealed him. (John 1)

This text is patterned after the creation story in Genesis (Ch. 1), and also the personification of Wisdom (Proverbs 8), quoted earlier. Jesus is this personification of wisdom made flesh. This is a poetic description of Jesus as teacher, but many Jews objected because John's emphasis seemed to make Moses second class or unimportant.

The New Testament did challenge some current Torah interpretations and practices, all of which had been given the weight of Moses' authority, but the intent was not to deny the validity of the Law or Moses. The original idea was to reform the religion rather than replace it. The important point here is that the Covenant concept was not abandoned by the Christians. Their way of life was built around it, based on the teachings of Jesus. It was an important anchor orienting the new movement.

It is true that some early Christians wanted more radical change or even an entirely new approach. Marcion, for example, an influential second century theologian, threw out the entire Old Testament and created a religion based mostly on Paul's writings. And there were some influential Gnostics, claiming to be Christian, who rejected the Law and its moral teachings altogether as they instituted orgiastic "freedom" rituals that became the embarrassment of the orthodox Church. But the

Christian movement as a whole did not dismiss the Old Testament. In emphasizing faith in Jesus over the Law, Paul probably made the most extreme statements in the New Testament, but even he accepted the Law as coming from God. He grew up studying it as a Pharisee and practiced it as a Christian. However, after his conversion he no longer conformed to it in a rigid, legalistic manner. He belongs with the other New Testament figures and Church Fathers who retained the Old Testament with its Ten Commandments as central components of Christian religion.

Paul's gospel of freedom led some to abandon the moral constraints of Mosaic Law based on the fantasy that Christian freedom allowed people to do whatever they wanted, without limitation. But Paul rejected this. The Old Law had been superseded by the Gospel but was still God's revelation. Perfect Christians were guided by the Spirit and did not need the Law to live the new life of freedom, but how many perfect Christians were there? The new faith was radical indeed, and because of its energy and power, most Christians required direction. The orientation needed was provided by the Old Testament, interpreted in accord with the teachings of Jesus.

The New Testament is filled with references to Jesus as prophet, wise man and healer, all of which are teaching roles. Moral lessons abound in his Sermon on the Mount, parables, cures and speeches. Similar lessons are given by Peter, Paul and other disciples. James, in his letter, presents moral instructions in the style of the wisdom teachers of old. In one place, he recognizes the need for teachers, but insists that they be of high quality.

> Not many of you should become teachers, my brothers…
> All of us fall short in many respects….If one of you is
> wise and understanding, let him show this in practice
> through a humility filled with good sense. Should you
> instead nurse bitter jealousy and selfish ambition in your

hearts, at least refrain from arrogant and false claims against the truth.

Wisdom like this does not come from above. (James 3)

True wisdom comes from above, from "the Father of Lights," as James says. It is not found among ignorant, self-absorbed or worldly-wise instructors.

These Law and Gospel instructions have influenced human thinking for thousands of years. The Founders learned from them, as well as from later history and their own experience, that a healthy society requires good education based on wise discipline, and that providing it is a never-ending task. The Bible warns again and again against forgetting the wisdom of the past; yet Israel did so generation after generation. And here we are today, doing it again. We are quickly forgetting three thousand years of educational experience, including the best of an American tradition that is only a few years old by comparison.

The Founders' Approach Today

The Founders' approach could be a useful meditation for today's progressive revisionists in education and government. The question to be considered is: what is the goal of "progress"? If it changes or dismantles our cultural and political traditions, what will follow? Will people still know the basics of democratic society? Equality and fairness may be sought, but how are they to be attained if the methods employed result in cultural ignorance? This is a major concern but it does not seem to bother revisionists. In fact, it seems to be what they desire. The trend for many years has been to move away from traditional ideas and practices in education and government in order to encounter less resistance as new approaches are initiated. But without historical perspective there is little insight regarding long-term results. Ad hoc solutions abound while long term implications are ignored. Inevitably, those implications will become more apparent if the nation continues to drift away from its historical moorings and becomes disoriented. Social cohesion will then most likely be maintained by ever-stronger governmental control, as has often happened in the past.

Russian history offers an example. Communist revolutionaries wanted a fresh start. A new social order required ending the old one, so they did away with the tsars and indoctrinated youth with socialist ideas. They also tried to eradicate traditional religion and its insistence on obeying God rather than man. Removing the tsars eliminated the old political regime and opened the door for socialist education and planning, but abolishing religion proved to be more difficult. Beliefs in the primacy of personal conscience and the virtues of faith caused people to resist submitting to atheistic authorities. Religious practices were suppressed and atheistic teachings were promoted, but despite all the new teachings, plans and programs, promised freedoms did not materialize. On the contrary, they were lost as central authority gained power and became despotic.

These events unfolded in our time, but in essence they reenacted an old story. The makers of our Constitution knew from history that initial hopes for a better world could end in despotism. They also knew that failure to learn from past experience would almost guarantee the reoccurrence of tyranny. Their foresight is noteworthy when considering the innovative nature of the American Revolution. The Founders wanted a new political structure based on people-power, but not one that dismissed the age-old institutions of public justice. They relied heavily on the wisdom of the religious and political traditions of the past to give the new government stability and focus. The Bible, as well as English, Scottish and French precedents were especially relevant. These sources helped them avoid the extremes of either dictatorship or mob rule.

CHAPTER 7

Contemporary Ideas

Those who maintain that education should prepare one for living successfully in this world have won a practically complete victory....The prevailing conception is that education must be such as will enable one to acquire enough wealth to live on the plane of the bourgeoisie.

That kind of education does not develop the aristocratic virtues. It neither encourages reflection nor inspires a reverence for the good. (Richard Weaver)

T his statement may surprise people now as much as it did in 1948 when Dr. Weaver wrote it. The overriding assumption for years has been that the primary purpose of education is job preparation for the accumulation of wealth. But Weaver had another view. He and others, including the Founding Fathers, believed that education has a more important function. Just after World War II, Weaver wrote *Ideas Have Consequences,* a book about current trends in education and culture. At a time when people were still celebrating victory over the Axis powers, Weaver was pointing out that a fundamental problem remained after the War. It was not solved by conquering our enemies on the battlefield because their fanaticism was a symptom rather than a cause of the War.

The disintegration of cultural beliefs in the West, combined with the lethal power of modern weapons, had produced destruction on a scale unknown to history. The reason this was possible, he said, was not only because of military might and political extremism. More fundamental was the idea that large numbers of people had about themselves and their goals. Certainly not everyone believed that world domination was the ultimate goal of life, or that confiscating other people's property was the way to happiness, but those who did were able to lead whole populations into military conflicts that resulted in international havoc.

Weaver saw the problem in terms of human knowledge. The ideas people live by produce concomitant actions. If the prevailing ideas of a group are dismissive or hateful toward other groups, or if they believe material wealth and power create ultimate satisfaction, accordant actions are foreseeable. Behavior follows ideas, and ideas have consequences.

Weaver wrote this book because he thought that the basic causes of the War were still at work. People were still thinking as they had earlier about material benefits as ends in themselves, and showing the same willingness to give up control of their personal lives to acquire wealth and comfort. He saw that these are fundamental errors – human freedom does not depend on externals; it depends on the willingness of individuals to believe in themselves and develop their capabilities for productive living (Weaver, 51, 73). The key to true success is personal self-control and the pursuit of higher ends than external riches. When that belief is lost, freedom is lost. People then are willing to give up personal rights for the sake of material gain. Weaver's conviction was that "the only guarantee against external control...is self-discipline". (Weaver, 91)

The main problem Weaver saw was ignorance of the true foundation of freedom. The aristocratic virtues he described were not elitist qualities possessed only by the privileged; they were basic moral values espoused by western religion for all humans. He saw that it is the task of education to foster the knowledge and practice of those virtues.

His view is consistent with traditional Christian teaching about the nature and purpose of human life. The materialistic notion he rejected is based on a non-religious or atheistic concept of man. If humans are no more than tangible matter, their needs and goals must be of the same nature. But if they are more than that, a broader view is required. Christian theology has dealt with this subject in great detail over the centuries. The main premise is that the bodily dimension is only part of the human makeup; there are also rational and spiritual elements involved.

An excellent summary of this outlook is found in the work of William of St. Thierry, a brilliant Cistercian monk who studied and taught medicine, physiology, philosophy and theology. He characterized humans as being composed of body, mind and spirit. The body, or "animal man," as he put it, is concerned about all things material. He lives in the realm of the tangible world and perceives his needs in those terms. This is not an unnatural condition; it is the normal state of infants and youngsters. But it becomes a problem if it continues to be dominant in adulthood. The adult "animal man" is still focused on basic bodily needs and desires. "His god is his belly," as St. Paul said. He fears losing material benefits and is disposed to give allegiance to authorities who provide or promise to provide material security. He only dimly suspects a higher form of existence but can advance if he has the will to do so. If he does, he will begin to sense a higher reality not governed by materialism and external authority. In time he can reach the level of the "rational man," where he can basically rule himself. He is still under legitimate human authorities, but is primarily led by his own mental powers and conscience. If he chooses to do so, he is then capable of advancing to the level of the "spiritual man," aware of the unseen spiritual world and able to live with wisdom and love (William, *The Golden Epistle; Three Treatises on Man*).

This is a natural progression, said William, but it can be interrupted or thwarted by misplaced desires. One of these is the desire to remain in the comfort zone of the first level. Such a person is especially susceptible to false ideas and promises of material gain. Dr. Weaver's outlook is quite similar. He understood that this condition is unhealthy and can become a major problem when it is compounded by power-hungry figures who try to keep people in this state. They may be able to do this by force but more often by propaganda and by providing material benefits that satisfy the body but not the mind. The rational powers are then not developed and people remain dependent. They are trained to obey and to pursue materialistic goals, with little attention to intellectual development or to moral and spiritual values.

Such a materialistic and anti-intellectual plan was behind the Nazis and Russian Communist drive for domination. It was far more powerful than was recognized at the time and ended by eventually devastating Europe. Weaver realized that the same patterns of thought were developing in America. He believed that it was the task of education to make citizens aware of this trend and to counteract it by encouraging self-reliance and intellectual development. It is the same path to freedom that was promoted by the Founding Fathers.

The Schools and Moral Teaching

Early Americans considered an education designed for democracy to be essential for its survival, and its centerpiece was moral education. Many of their writings attest to this. Today, however, this American idea is being severely tested by secular and anti-religious elements. Much of this is revealed in government involvements with education. Although schools would be better, and society would benefit if moral character was emphasized in education, we find that the opposite has happened. Not only has that purpose of learning been supplanted; it is being actively opposed by those who object to such teaching because of the religious connotations associated with many moral ideas.

At stake is a question of policy, not necessarily the efforts of individual educators. No doubt there are many competent instructors in the schools and colleges who embody honorable moral standards and lead by example, but they do not reflect the national educational atmosphere as a whole. Traditional moral teaching is no longer a priority. Unlike the early days when Bible instruction was commonplace, today's public education forbids it. The usual argument is based on so-called First Amendment violations, even though it is far removed from the intentions of the writers of the Constitution. Their intention was to ensure the freedom of religious expression rather than to suppress it, as is the current practice. Respect for non-believers was guaranteed even though the moral values our Founders encouraged were Christian or Judeo-Christian. To forbid such teachings in schools would no doubt be incomprehensible to them.

This is not to say that moral teachings are absent in today's schools. Values of one kind or another are always present in that teachers, professors and administrators inevitably reveal their own attitudes to students, intentionally or not. Some current viewpoints are worthwhile, as, for example, those encouraging environmental awareness, provided the subject is approached scientifically and not politically. But when teachings ignore or question such values as patriotism, family life, the work ethic and religious expression, our western moral-religious tradition is undermined.

THE COURTS

Education and the Secular Courts

In recent years traditional values have come under serious attack in schools, political venues, social media and the courts. One would think that in our schools, a good education would foster methods of learning that are time-tested, but it has become clear that behind the upheaval caused by new approaches is a determined effort to completely revamp education in a secularist mode (See *A Note on Secularism* on page 51-53). But is this what the people want, or is this sea change in educational philosophy instead being led by a relatively small segment of the population? It is not likely that the majority of Americans want a religionless, "value-free" school system. Not only would such a system be alien to our history, it would undermine the concept of democratic freedom we have known since revolutionary days.

The new morality, instead of encouraging self-reliance and moral strength, advocates action based on subjective feelings, individual satisfaction and personal autonomy. But how has this change come about? One factor, and perhaps the major one, has been the success the secularist element has had in overcoming the religious-moral viewpoint, not by superior reasoning, evidence or popular demand, but by gaining control of educational unions and bureaucracies, and by employing the powers of the courts.

Many court cases involve education, particularly in regard to church-state relations. Whereas government in earlier times encouraged religious teaching and often supported it financially, today this precedent is ignored. For example, as mentioned earlier, under Jefferson Catholic missions to the Indians were given financial aid, as were other religious activities until the end of the nineteenth century, when aid to sectarian schools was terminated because of the high costs involved (Levin, 40). In our day, the courts have sometimes completely reversed the thinking of the Founders by declaring unconstitutional practices that had been commonplace earlier. A landmark case was *Everson v. Board of Education* (1947), which brought Jefferson's "wall of separation" metaphor into the lexicon of modern jurists. Although the Court let stand a New Jersey policy of providing bus fare for students in sectarian as well as public schools, the opinion of Justice Hugo Black decreed that the First Amendment applies not only to the Federal government, but also to states and localities. In doing this, he used the "wall" metaphor, not as Jefferson meant it, but in the opposite sense – the protection of government from religion.

In more recent times the courts have intervened repeatedly in the affairs of the people and the rights of parents to educate their children as they wish by using *Everson* as a precedent. In *Engel v. Vitale* (1962), for example, the court declared unconstitutional a simple non-denominational prayer composed by the New York State Board of Regents which was recited each day in the schools. It said:

Almighty God, we acknowledge our dependence upon Thee,

and we beg Thy blessings upon us, our parents, our teachers,

and our Country.

The Court somehow determined that this was an attempt to establish a religion and therefore a violation of the First Amendment. Many lower courts have followed along in this reasoning, resulting in the elimination of practically all religious references in the schools and public places. Some later Supreme Court decisions did narrowly favor religious expression, but the harm had been done and continues to be done in public education.

Some justices themselves have acknowledged the inaccuracy of this precedent. Chief Justice Rehnquist once stated that "it is impossible to build sound constitutional doctrine upon a mistaken understanding of constitutional history, expressly freighted with Jefferson's misleading metaphor for nearly forty years." He also said, "the 'wall of separation between church and state' is a metaphor based on bad history, a metaphor which has proven useless as a guide to judging. It should be frankly and explicitly abandoned" (Levin, 44-45).

Not only should it be abandoned, it should be made clear that the education of children is the right and obligation of parents and not the courts. For the courts or any branch of government to dictate curriculum as they do when preventing non-sectarian religious and moral instruction is to upset the balance of powers envisioned by the Constitution. We must ask who should have primary responsibility here. Is it the parents and people of the community or government functionaries far from the classroom?

Government Interference: A Judge
Judges "Intelligent Design"

A case in point is the recent decision by federal judge John E. Jones that declared unconstitutional a Pennsylvania school board policy to have a statement read in biology class concerning "intelligent design." The statement, read once at the beginning of the ninth-grade biology unit, states that "Because Darwin's theory is a theory, it continues to be tested as new evidence is discovered…Intelligent Design is an explanation of the origin of life that differs from Darwin's view," and names a reference book for students who might be interested. "With respect to any theory," it continues, "students are encouraged to keep an open mind." The course then teaches Darwin, not Intelligent Design. The judge called the board's decision to have this statement read "breathtaking inanity" and a conscious attempt to promote religion, in violation of church-state separation (Jones, 138; Sataline).

Objections to this ruling have arisen due to some puzzling features about it. One is that it claims a statement that questions, but does not deny, a scientific opinion is a violation of the First Amendment. But this seems to assume that the right of free speech, also enshrined in that Amendment, does not protect the right to present views that question an assumed "correct" opinion. The claim is that the alternate view is not "scientific" because religious motivations are suspected. But one would think that the principle of free speech should allow challenges to any opinion, including scientific ones. After all, scientists do it all the time, even where supposed scientific "facts" are at issue. Some go far beyond accepted scientific opinions to conclusions or suggestions unavailable to tangible measurement.

Any accepted scientific idea is subject to revision and sometimes to radical change. There are views on astronomy and physics that cannot be supported by direct physical evidence. The Big Bang, dark matter, parallel universes, the structure and movement of atoms and a host of other matters are constantly under review. Yet evolution, as currently understood, is treated as sacrosanct dogma. If a challenging presentation becomes proselytizing, it should not be allowed in public schools, but if it concerns the issue of evolution itself, there should be no cause for it be censured. The religious beliefs of those presenting alternate views should have nothing to do with it. In this case the alternate view was condemned as a violation of the Constitution even though it was not taught.

There is also the question of whether a federal judge should have the right to dictate what can or cannot be taught in a local biology class. What power does the Constitution give him that allows him to intervene in local educational affairs of this kind? The First Amendment as written refers to acts of Congress, and even though it has recently been applied to the States, does not specify separation of church and state in a manner that supports government interference of this kind.

Another issue concerns the expertise the judge has in biology – and religion – that qualifies him to make his determination. Even if it could be shown he has jurisdiction in this affair, the question is whether he should exercise it in the absence of competent knowledge of the scientific-philosophical-theological issues involved. He depends on the opinions of science experts in this case. But local parents and school officials could do the same thing and make their own judgment. The judge could have taken this opportunity to remove the federal court from the case based on lack of competence and jurisdiction. It could have been seen as a local issue to be resolved locally instead of one that concerns the federal government. One may also wonder why the establishment clause of the First Amendment is employed in the decision, but not the free speech clause.

Regarding this case, even though religion is a motivating factor, it is not clear that religion should be at issue at all, inasmuch as "intelligent design" relates to a scientific theory and questions gaps in evidence and assumptions drawn from the data. If objections are to be made, they can be based on science, not religious motivation. The discussion in biology class could focus on the scientific evidence or lack of it, as well as challenges to the evidence and conclusions drawn from it. The entire issue can be handled on the playing field of science without engaging in theological terminology. If some scientists and secularists want to infer definitive meaning from the evidence, they can do so without insisting on the only or final say in a matter that goes beyond the available scientific evidence. Others should have a right to speak as well.

Other Examples of Secular Bias

Another recent case involved Steven Williams, a fifth-grade teacher in Cupertino, California, who was forbidden to distribute documents to his students because of their religious content. Among the forbidden documents were excerpts from the Declaration of Independence and writings by George Washington, Samuel Adams and William Penn. Administrators said these materials were "inappropriate" for eleven-year-olds (Mesfin, A7). They also said that since these writings are of a religious nature they are not appropriate because the school honors separation of church and state (Boyer, 62f.). Mr. Williams was forced to sue to be allowed to present these historical documents in class ("Williams v. Vidmar, 2005").

We can be sure that George Washington, John Adams or Thomas Jefferson would have a problem with this. This was certainly not their idea of church-state separation. The "wall of separation" phrase often quoted today comes from a letter Jefferson wrote to a Baptist congregation in Connecticut regarding the freedom of religion. The Baptists feared that the state would suppress their church, as had been the case elsewhere, by requiring them to support and pay taxes to the Congregationalist Church as the official church of Connecticut. Jefferson agreed with them that all should be allowed to practice their religion freely, without state involvement or preference. The "wall" would protect every citizen from government interference and from attempts to establish an official church (Jefferson, *Letter of the Danbury Baptists & Jefferson's reply*). The point was not to keep religion out of government but to keep government out of religion. The "wall" metaphor had been used earlier by Roger Williams of Rhode Island in defense of religious freedom from government and was used in the same way by Jefferson. Nonetheless, it is given almost the opposite meaning today and used as constitutional justification for governmental interference in religious expression in education and other public forums.

Another example is a recent controversy between parents and the Scotts Valley, California high school over posters in the classrooms that promote the homosexual lifestyle. Parents who objected to this argued that they do not agree with this viewpoint, and that it is not balanced with alternative or traditional viewpoints. They believe their children should not be subjected to such controversial topics when no other viewpoints are allowed. Administrators and some faculty argued that the need for "diversity" and "tolerance" permit emphasis on non-traditional opinions, but not traditional ones, because of church-state separation (Tobin). At a public meeting on this, which filled the gym to overflowing, the school lawyer announced that this practice was in accord with state law, and since public schools are "creatures of the state" the parents had no right to object or remove their children from any class because of disagreement with the subject matter. One wonders how this is different from the forced educational policies of autocratic governments around the world.

This statement was not challenged, probably because it was not the immediate issue, but it could have been the subject of an intense debate. It is not at all clear that the nation has decided that schools belong to government officials rather than the local citizens. Taking authority for the curriculum away from local districts and giving it to government bureaucrats is a very serious matter. This subject requires a great deal of attention.

There have been numerous episodes of government high-handedness in recent times. In Iowa, in the 1960's, the Amish refused to send their children to public schools for religious reasons. The state Board of Education sued them for non-compliance with state regulations, even though the Amish taught their children at home and raised good and productive citizens. The Amish never broke laws, except this one, and were very successful farmers. The result was that the fines and penalties imposed by the state were so severe that they lost their farms. They left Iowa and moved to South America, where they could practice their religion freely.

The Constitution and the Uses of Power

The Constitution is designed to ensure freedom of the people from coercive government. It does this by instituting a political structure that separates power among legislative, executive and judicial branches, and rests on the premise that government exists to serve the people – not the other way around. Thus it prevents concentration of power in a king such as George III or in an elite class. Underlying constitutional thinking is the belief that human beings have the capacity to determine their own destiny, rather than depending on rulers to do that. It is rarely noted today, but well known to the Framers that this is a religious idea, rooted in the biblical notion of man as the image of God. Humans have physical, mental and spiritual strengths that allow them to make their own way in life, and although their imperfections require governments to serve the interests of justice, their rights and obligations take precedence over governmental power. Government exists by the consent of the people, which means that their rights are innate and not conferred by government.

The Constitution enumerates the powers of government and specifically states that all other powers are reserved to the states and the people (Amendments IX and X). The Declaration of Independence presents this concept in terms of the people's right to freedom, which "the Laws of Nature and Nature's God entitle them." Thus they are "endowed by their Creator" with the rights of life, liberty and the pursuit of happiness, and "to secure these Rights, Governments are instituted among Men, deriving their just Powers from the Consent of the Governed ...." This statement embodies the essence of the Founders' understanding of the dignity and capacities of human beings, and the legitimate relationship between them and government. It explains why the Federal government is divided between three branches and why the powers of those branches are limited by enumeration. We do not want excessive concentration of power, and we do not look to government to confer rights and freedoms; the people already have them as creatures of God rather than of the state.

Today we face an ongoing battle for power between the branches of government, and between them and the people at large. One of the most important battles for supremacy concerns the role of the Judiciary. Judges today have assumed powers over the people and other branches of government that would probably have astounded early Americans. But power struggles have been going on since the Revolution, and it seems that they will continue well into our future. It is no doubt the nature of a republic that this be the case. Our forebears were not perfect, nor were they able to produce a perfect government, but they did create conditions for unheard-of political freedoms. The fact that freedom was and continues to be difficult to achieve should not prevent us from carrying on their efforts to balance these powers in the best interests of the people.

It is becoming clear that the trend toward secularism in education is a direct threat to American constitutional liberty. It infringes on the power of people to solve their own problems and to live free of excessive government interference. All three branches of government are needed, but they serve democracy only when constrained and limited to their proper roles as servants rather than rulers of the people.

The enumeration in the Constitution

of certain rights shall not be construed

to deny or disparage others retained

by the people. (Amendment IX)

THE SCHOOLS

School Priorities and Funding Solutions

Parents believe in education, as do most Americans. This has always been the case although priorities have changed. Today funding is a major issue, whereas the Founders were much more concerned about the curriculum. The proof of this is the enormous amount of effort and time spent on money issues today in relation to the emphasis on general education. Yet the current approach has not satisfied us, and we continue to engage in seemingly endless impassioned debates over education. The reason is that the outcomes are not what we expect. There are a number of signs that student accomplishments are declining or, at best, not improving. Criticisms abound, as do proposed solutions, most of which involve additional funding. But if funding is the answer, how much more do we need to spend to solve the problem? Consider this: according to the U.S. Department of Education, in 2004-05, public and private education was estimated to cost Americans $536 billion for K-12 schooling and another $373 billion for higher education (U.S. Dept. of Education, "10 Facts"). Yet many thought that this $909 billion total was not enough.

How do we even imagine how much money that is? What is one "billion"? One billion minutes ago, the Roman Empire was ruling, and 909 billion minutes ago, humans hadn't yet appeared on the planet. One billion dollar bills laid end to end would span 94,697 miles, which is about 3.8 times around the earth. 909 billion would encircle the globe over 3400 times.

In 2004-05 the U.S. was heavily engaged in Iraq and Afghanistan. There were loud complaints that military spending in those campaigns was short-changing education. Proposals were made to redirect that military money to education. But the fact was that the U.S. spent more on education in that school year alone than was spent on both wars since 2001. From 2001 to 2008 Congress had approved about $700 billion for all military operations, military bases, foreign aid and veterans' health care. The CBO estimated that the total cost for Iraq, Afghanistan and the global war on terror could reach $1.1 to $1.7 trillion from 2001 to 2018 ("The Cost of Iraq"). In contrast, the government estimate for spending in the U.S. for all public and private education for the 2008-09 school year alone was over $1.1 trillion (U.S. Dept. of Education, "Digest"). A new study shows that support for increased school spending diminishes notably after people become aware of how much we are already spending (Peterson, A11).

The point of these comparisons is not to approve or defend war but to provide some perspective on education costs. They are astronomical by any standard, and it is difficult to imagine that they are not enough for American formal education. There must be enormous waste, inefficiency and misdirection of funds in the system to account for this, but even allowing for that, if funding was the answer to the education problem, one would think we would have solved it by now. Since we have not, it is time to look elsewhere for a solution.

Teachers who care about their students know that money alone is not the solution. The political, bureaucratic and union-dominated nature of public education, which often hinders the learning process, would not go away with additional funding, nor would it solve the basic instructional deficiencies of private schools. Rather than looking to funding as an answer, a more useful approach might be one that centers directly on the fundamentals of learning. To do that we must first take a look at what today's formal education is trying to do.

Parents, older students and most Americans see a good education as a pathway to a better life and are therefore willing to pay for it. But what exactly is a "good education"? No doubt for most people, it is one that provides adequate preparation for jobs. People go to school and send their children to school for a variety of reasons, including the 3 R's, socialization, baby-sitting, sports, science/humanities studies, and learning for its own sake, but above all is the hope that a good education will prepare students for jobs that help them make a living. This can be called "skills training," and it pervades education from learning the ABC's to advanced graduate studies. (The subject here is education as student-centered teaching, not as highly specialized and industrial research, which have become major priorities in many universities). Skills training is rarely challenged as the first priority of education; it is what people expect, and what employers expect in their search for employees with the basic skills needed to perform on the job. This is a worthy goal, but when employee training becomes the main focus of education, a fundamental flaw is exposed.

The Missing Element in Education

The money we are spending for education is not producing the results we want. Some see the cause in faulty allocation and misuse of funds and this is indeed a huge problem. With a trillion dollar budget, one would think teachers would not have to spend their own money to buy basic classroom supplies, or that school buildings could be dilapidated to the point of being unsafe to enter. At the same time, stories are appearing about administrators taking exorbitant salaries and bonuses. It is not surprising that taxpayers wonder where all that money goes. But even if these resources were efficiently employed, a "good education" would not necessarily follow because, as our Founders knew so well, money is not the main ingredient in quality education. Money devoted to skills training for job preparation is obviously important, but it very well may be that excessive focus on that actually makes it more difficult to achieve. This is because job training alone cannot achieve the true aims of education. Even more important is the discipline and moral purpose that encourages learning and social responsibility.

We often hear business executives bewailing the state of U. S. education because they cannot find enough students prepared to do the jobs their companies require. Some do more than complain and are trying to do something about it. For example, in the past ten years Intel has invested over one billion dollars to improve teaching and learning in the U.S and 70 other countries. Intel employees have volunteered about three million hours toward this effort. The company gives computers and technical training to students and is involved in numerous national and state programs for education, working with governors, education officials and other corporations. It provides programs for teaching/ learning assessment, curriculum standards, professional development, information technology and scientific research (Intel).

IBM is another company that has invested heavily in education worldwide. It offers a large number of programs covering everything from kids' computers for reading to advanced university research. Since 1998 IBM has provided 50,000 computers to 10 million children, as well as several web-based reading courses. It conducts science camps and many courses in technical training. In 2010 alone IBM spent $100 million for grants and research in universities (IBM).

These activities, apart from the support for specialized research that directly benefits the companies, are features of a commitment to corporate responsibility. They are laudable efforts and we may assume that they are of high quality. No doubt they also aid company efforts to recruit employees skilled in math, science and technology. While recognizing the good they do, however, it must be said that they are not designed to educate citizens in the way our Founders envisioned. They are part of the solution, but by no means all of it. The reading programs can benefit all students regardless of future employment, but the overall intent of the programs is aimed at preparing students for jobs requiring skills in math, science and technology – those areas of particular interest to companies seeking qualified employees. No doubt history, literature, philosophy or other academic disciplines get less attention. This is not a criticism; these programs do what they are intended to do, but they must not be regarded as models for American education as a whole. Being primarily oriented toward job training in the world of technology, they lack emphasis on what early leaders thought was more important, i.e., the overall meaning of American citizenship. As such they are not a cure for education's more fundamental problems, which are on the level of personal development and civic responsibility. The form of government envisioned by the Constitution sets a high priority on preparing a broadly and morally educated citizenry.

Great emphasis is now being placed on math and science in American schools, in line with the business-technology model. New efforts are being made to employ technological tools for learning (video games, internet and computer applications, communication innovations, etc.). If successful, technological skills and job opportunities could improve. But unless this emphasis is accompanied by equal emphasis on personal discipline and moral purpose, it might still be difficult to find students who are interested and motivated enough to become competent employees. Students may be fascinated by new technologies, but if they become nothing more than novelties that are fun and make studying easier, they will not aid development of the technical skills needed in the workplace. For students who do apply themselves, a different problem arises. Morally unguided technical education opens the door to misuse of skills such as we are now experiencing with computer hackers.

Money, power and fame are also motives for learning, but they may not produce long-range benefits to the company or to society. Even highly trained employees with good intentions may fall into irresponsible uses of learned skills if their focus is too narrow and their moral perspective too weakly developed. If a person uses a saw, drill or some other power tool without knowing or paying attention to the safety instructions, bad things can happen. In the case of technical and business enterprises, if sophisticated intellectual tools are employed without knowledge or attention to ethical guidelines and social responsibility, extremely bad things can happen. How do we know that advanced engineering, technological and business skills will be used wisely? We may not even think this is a valid question. But ethical guidelines surely have a place in business, politics, medicine, law, science and technology.

At one time, it was not uncommon for scientists and engineers to say that their job was to concentrate on their projects, and not be concerned about the social implications. How their technology would be used was not their problem or responsibility. That attitude may have diminished somewhat after WWII, when the results of atomic research on the bomb, Nazi lab experiments on human beings and other uses of technology became known. More recently, doubts have been raised about research on animals as well as humans, and about the technological causes of environmental problems. However, although there is now heightened awareness of such dangers, the specialized education of technology students and other professionals has not changed much in regard to the moral dimension. We continue to push for more and better technology and sophisticated business techniques, but not for the kind of education that would help students understand their work in a broader framework.

Technological Solutions

An important aspect of contemporary education reform movements, aside from money issues, is the tendency to think mainly in terms of scientific training, technological tools and organizational structure. This emphasis is hardly questioned now, but it would probably have been seriously questioned by our Founders. While they would no doubt see the importance of such training, they might be more concerned about its tendency to overshadow the need for the general education of the citizenry. They could see this shift in priorities as having unsettling ramifications for the democratic nation they established.

Consider the effects of this trend from an historical standpoint. An example of current approaches is a proposal by Louis Gerstner, former CEO of IBM. He has a genuine interest in better education and has written and spoken about education's problems for years. He is "worried about what [they] will mean for our future workforce." He has offered several suggestions on how to improve job training in schools. They include setting higher academic standards, paying good teachers better, measuring and testing teacher/student performance and imposing a longer school year. These are not new ideas; they have been goals of reformers for years. But Mr. Gerstner also has a plan to abolish all local school districts and establish a national organization for creating the curriculum and hiring the teachers. This supposedly would allow his other ideas to be implemented (Gerstner).

Mr. Gerstner says he has been working at school reform for 40 years. Reform is certainly needed, and he should be acknowledged for recognizing this and working to improve schools. But his proposal raises some difficult questions:

Is it fair to ask how much of his advice is based on the need to prepare all students for living in a democratic society? Does it deal with many of the day-to-day teaching challenges caused by the narrow interests of some aggressive parents, politicians and government officials, or by TV and movie influences, excessive individualism, drug and alcohol use, conditions of affluence or poverty and other local matters that affect education? There are many concerned people, aware of the current state of education and of these cultural problems, who have attempted to make improvements but have been thwarted by a host of obstacles. More than a few of these obstacles have been created by government intervention, yet Mr. Gerstner is proposing government control as a solution.

It is an open question whether a national program would have any more success than local programs have had. State and federal involvement is heavy already, yet education does not improve. In California, for example, the State already dictates the curriculum and the qualifications for teachers. Moving that jurisdiction even farther away from localities to Washington would not necessarily help. Instead of doubling-down on an ineffective policy, we might stop to consider the real possibility that more government intrusion could actually make matters worse. Gerstner would put national experts and the U.S. Department of Education in charge of the system. They would assign the curriculum and hire teachers. But this would be a massive undertaking on a national scale, and would assume that these administrators could somehow be more successful than the ones we now have.

State and federal authorities who now have extensive input into local school affairs are considered educational "experts," yet their track record is nothing to be envied. Adding to or replacing them would not guarantee that they would be able to deal effectively with the problem. Gerstner thinks we have too many bureaucratic agencies in education, which is true, but even one agency could quickly be filled with political appointees with limited understanding of the real needs of education and little knowledge of local circumstances throughout the nation. Excessive government intervention was a problem the Founders feared.

Examples of how the federal government runs education projects are found in national job training programs for youth and the unemployed, authorized by Congress since 1962. Several have been created over the years, each to correct the errors of earlier ones, but with little success. Some studies show that these programs actually reduced job prospects and earning power of participants. As of 2011, there were 47 different federal training programs, run at a cost of $18 billion a year, with little or no evidence that they do any good and some evidence that they actually increase unemployment. In 2008 the Department of Health and Human Services began tracking 5,000 three- and four-year-olds in the Head Start program through third grade. The results, reported in October, 2012, showed no measurable improvement in performance of these students over those not in the program. Head Start began in 1965 and has cost over $180 billion to operate. The outcomes have been more than disappointing (Burke and Muhlhausen). Some more recent programs have shown promise, but these, for the most part, are privately operated (Bovard, A17).

Mr. Gerstner is worried about preparing students for his industry, and other businesses as well. This raises another question: why should taxpayers and anyone else outside a particular company or industry be responsible for training their employees? We are so accustomed to think of education as job training that it is almost unheard of to even raise this question. But there is a difference between quality general education, which is and always has been the responsibility of all Americans, and technical training for specific jobs. Up to now, we have assumed that preparation for highly technical work should be done in our schools and colleges, but there is a limit to how much society in general is responsible for preparing students for particular business needs. Interest in improving public and private education is commendable, but it should not be limited to special needs that overshadow the importance of general education for all citizens. All students need basic reading, math and science, but not all need to be trained as engineers, scientists or business executives.

Businesses already provide a good amount of special training for employees, and it may be necessary to provide more, given the state of public education and the constantly changing business and social environment. Perhaps efforts to help public schools would be better directed toward general education, which, if done well, will develop the skills needed to understand and deal effectively with the changing conditions of our time. The basic reading, math and science programs already in the curriculums of Intel, IBM and other businesses could be useful contributions to this overall effort.

There seems to be a growing realization that technical training alone is insufficient. Some in the business world are realizing the value of general education (White, B4). Norm Augustine, former CEO of Lockheed Martin, has found that general education, particularly in historical studies, prepares engineers for their work better than concentration on math and science alone. He says that the broadly educated worker is becoming an increasingly important part of the quest for economic productivity and growth (Augustine; also see Berkowitz).

Technical training is not the only area of concern. Education programs in business, law, medicine and other areas affecting the general population also minimize historical and moral instruction. Courses are given in ethics, but these requirements may be offered and taken half-heartedly. Professors have admitted feeling unprepared or uninterested in teaching in this area, and students may see it as unnecessary and a waste of time. Even those interested could find the courses insufficient to deal with any issue in depth. To make moral teaching worthwhile, more than a few elective or required courses are needed. If it is to have any lasting effect, moral education must become an integral part of the entire curriculum through such things as team-teaching, interdisciplinary studies and the strong commitment of administrators.

The criticism we hear is valid; students generally are not well prepared for today's workplace, but the underlying reason for this is not being addressed by most current reform proposals. From an historical viewpoint, more important than any of the best-known solutions now being offered is the need to develop a true sense of human capability and the meaning of citizenship, with the mental and physical disciplines required to learn and be productive in any work setting. Many current trends in education do almost the opposite. They de-emphasize these values and focus on particular areas – math, computer and lab sciences, and business techniques – almost as ends in themselves. These courses can be quite rigorous and can appeal to better students, but they crowd out other areas of knowledge. They belong in particular major and graduate programs, but are not sufficiently combined or integrated with traditional academic disciplines.

The thinking is that there is not enough time to cover these other areas, nor is there sufficient interest in doing so. But while the current practice may produce at least some highly trained graduates, they come out of this experience narrowly educated and unprepared to deal with the complex moral issues they must certainly face in their employment. Important ethical questions may not even occur to them regarding relations with co-workers and customers, the quality of products and services and the social implications of their work. Above all is the neglect of the requirements of citizenship.

There are exceptions, but in most schools something is missing in the educational experience, and it is not money or government involvement. Substandard scientific and technical proficiency is not the basic problem either. Rather, it is the abandonment of educational principles developed over thousands of years that endeavor to attune the learning experience to the actual natural faculties of human beings. Instead of building on this store of wisdom, as our Founders did, many educators today ignore or reject it. Some do this intentionally in order to promote secular, non-traditional values, while others may do it simply because new ideas seem more practical. But in either case, these untested notions create uncertain and often weak results. They deprive education of established principles that may not be perfect, but do provide a solid foundation for learning. These notions, now considered old-fashioned, are the result of generations of teaching experience and, properly understood, are the building blocks of future genuine reform and improvement in teaching. Future analysis will likely show that by neglecting these principles educators will lose touch with them, only to someday rediscover and resurrect them as surprisingly innovative and effective means of instruction.

University Priorities

Regarding the funding emphasis, there is a disconcerting inclination to fund highly specialized research and commercial ventures that benefit the university and some professors but have little to do with the education of most students. Universities claim they need more money for their teaching mission, but money that could go to undergraduate teaching is now being redirected to expensive and narrowly focused research programs. This enhances university prestige and generates income from patents and licenses, but shifts attention away from undergraduate programs and the general education of all students.

After the Bayh-Dole Act of 1980 was passed, public universities were allowed to own patents and enter into commercial ventures. Since then, research for these purposes has increased and in recent years has become a driving force in university growth all over the nation. Research universities are moving into this area aggressively by securing patents, licensing products and developing business start-up agreements.

Universities that do this gain recognition and prestige as research centers, but even more important to them may be the income produced by research license fees. The number of university-owned patents has risen dramatically in recent years. Since 1993 over 34,000 patents have been issues to universities, with the University of California leading the nation over the past several years. Nationwide, this is becoming a significant source of university funding. The figure is now well over $1.5 billion annually. Among the leaders in license fee income in 2009 were Northwestern University ($162 million), Columbia University ($154 million), New York University ($113 million) and the University of California ($103 million) (Petulla; AUTM).

To compete in this research game, universities pay enormous salaries to prestigious faculty and those able to do patentable research; in some cases over $1 million per year. Instructors of undergraduates, on the other hand, may make as little as $35,000 to $40,000, and graduate teaching assistants even less.

Universities throughout the nation are feverishly seeking funding, much of it going into specialized research. It seems difficult to justify this trend in terms of traditional educational goals. The time and effort devoted to funding technical research easily conflicts with interest in general education, regardless of university claims to be able to do both equally well. The president of the University of Chicago recently said that he was forced to engage in a $2 billion fund-raising campaign in order to compete with other major universities for research faculty and resources. The competition, he said, was fierce.

Columbia University offers an example of the aggressive attitude existing in research universities. In 2000, Columbia was facing the loss of a group of patents that had generated nearly $100 million annually for seventeen years. To protect that income stream, Columbia somehow managed to get a new patent for essentially the same thing. A number of drug companies who had been paying license fees for the old patents refused to continue paying because the "new" patent was not actually new. Lawsuits followed. The drug companies said the differences between these patents were miniscule. The new terms amounted to nothing more than synonyms for the old patent terms. It was like trying to get a new patent for a mouse trap by calling it a rodent trap. Also, the judge wondered how this "non-profit" institution could afford so many lawyers to argue their case. Fearing a loss, Columbia withdrew from the suit, at least temporarily. Nonetheless, license income continued to come in from patents. Figures vary year to year, but in 2003 Columbia made over $178 million in patent license income (Wysocki, A1).

Many schools are entering into business arrangements with private industry through joint ownership of project research and by selling licenses and stocks. Stanford made $336 million in 2005 by selling Google stock it owned as part of a research deal. Stanford now even has its own brand-name technology product. The University of Washington met a $2 billion fundraising goal seventeen months early in 2007 and then extended the campaign to reach another $500 million for engineering, medicine and business. The University of Chicago created ARCH Development Corporation to encourage new start-ups based on faculty research. MIT, Indiana University, Rice, the University of Minnesota, the University of Missouri, to mention a few, now have venture capital start-up programs (Buckman, B1; Herrick, B6). One may wonder how any of this relates to the education of most citizens.

These activities closely resemble those of private commercial enterprises in that research knowledge is not shared, as might be expected from educational institutions. In fact, university patents are closely guarded secrets. As early as 1985 Harvard upset other universities and companies by licensing a genetic mouse research project exclusively to DuPont. This prevented other scientists from working in the area while ensuring license income to Harvard. Baylor College of Medicine did the same thing with its genetic mouse research, licensing it exclusively to a private company. Access to the University of Wisconsin's breakthrough stem cell research was held exclusively by the Geron Corporation in California until university and government pressure convinced Wisconsin to soften some of the licensing requirements so that others could work on this taxpayer-funded research (Washburn, 151; Regalido and Hamilton, B1).

The resources needed for specialized research and commercial enterprises are enormous and can easily overshadow attention to general education. To illustrate, Yoshihiro Kawaoka, who does flu virus research at the University of Wisconsin, recently received an offer from the University of Pittsburgh worth over $20 million for salaries and lab facilities in a new $200 million biomedical research building. Because reputation, patents and licenses were at stake, Wisconsin scoured accounts throughout the University for a year before finding sufficient funds to keep him (Penn, 20f.). Admittedly, this man does valuable work, but he does not teach, except by directing a few assistants. His work probably would be much the same if he were employed by Merck or Eli Lilly. The point is that this corporate-style research in universities competes with resources for general education. Most students are totally removed from it, and it draws funds away from their areas of study. It means less contact with professors and more with temporary instructors. Meanwhile, tuition and fees steadily increase.

These are high-profile examples, but they represent a trend that heavily favors specialized research over undergraduate teaching. Recruitment/tenure/advancement criteria (publish or perish practices, publication records of new hires and existing faculty) within the university have been problems for years in this regard, and now commercial involvements are coming to the fore. This new focus does generate some scientific advancements but it does not enhance the prospects for general education, which is the critical need our Founders foresaw. We are quickly forgetting Madison's view, noted earlier, that colleges and universities were needed to train teachers for the nation. "They are the nurseries of skilful Teachers for the schools distributed throughout the Community....Without such Institutions...none but the few whose wealth enables them to support their sons abroad can give them the fullest education..." (Madison, *Letter to Barry*).

The Quality of Teaching

Henry George, a well-known economist, once gave a lecture to University of California faculty and students. On the subject of education he said:

> For the study of political economy, you need no special knowledge, no extensive library, no costly laboratory.
> You do not even need textbooks and teachers, if you will but think for yourselves....
>
> All this array of professors, all this paraphernalia of learning cannot educate a man. Here you may obtain tools; but they will be useful only to him who can use them. A monkey with a microscope, a mule packing a library, are fit emblems of the men – unfortunately there are plenty – who pass through the whole educational machinery and come out but learned fools, crammed with knowledge that they cannot use.... (George)

Professor George put his finger on a major weakness of modern education. Great stores of facts are presented in a piecemeal, unconnected way while traditional subjects and ideas are ignored. To compound the problem, students are taught to accept current social and political opinions as unassailable rather than to reflect on alternatives and think for themselves. Valid intellectual debates are sometimes replaced by polemical, one-sided lectures, shouting matches, sit-ins, building takeovers and belligerent demonstrations. But the unfortunate result of all this indoctrination and mob action for the universities is that parents, students and taxpayers are beginning to question the value of this sort of "education." A telltale sign of dissatisfaction with current trends in education is the declining public financial support for universities. One reason for this, of course, is that taxpayers are tapped out while education costs have skyrocketed. But there is also growing disenchantment with the questionable quality of instruction in some schools.

It must be emphasized that problems of this kind are not universal. There are probably many colleges, particularly smaller ones, that still strive to provide high quality basic education. An example is Hillsdale College (founded in1844) where historic American ideas and values have been taught since before the Civil War. Students there are required to take a number of basic core courses, including American history, and all must learn the Constitution in detail. The fact that this is unusual should give us pause.

It should also be noted that while large research universities have other interests, good teaching can be found there as well. Purdue University (1869), for example, was founded as a land-grant school to teach agriculture and engineering to settlers in the area. Although it did not have a broad-based curriculum originally, it has expanded the course offerings and departments to a large degree. It is known for producing competent graduates in many areas.

No doubt almost every school has faculty members who take teaching seriously, and some who try to educate students according to historical priorities. The problem is that these priorities are being replaced by other interests and it is becoming more difficult for schools to maintain first-rate teaching as their top concern.

Those universities and colleges who claim to be educational institutions with teaching as a first or high priority fail when they give only lip service to the national need for an educated citizenry. General education according to long-established American principles cannot be measured by total numbers of courses offered or degrees granted. The real sign of success is found in students' understanding of ideas and their applications to work, community and to life in general. General education opens the door to a broader and more informed worldview and helps develop the art of good judgment. It becomes especially valuable in personal, social, political and economic circumstances that all students will encounter, regardless of occupation. Teaching in this area requires in-depth scholarship combined with good communication skills, but appreciation for this work has waned as the curriculum has fragmented into more specialized and isolated pieces.

A case in point is the University of California at Santa Cruz (UCSC). It was founded in the 1960's as a classical liberal arts school in the pattern of Cambridge and Oxford, with small classes and extensive interaction between students and faculty. The idea was to counterbalance the trends in major universities that were moving away from emphasis on undergraduate teaching toward narrowly specialized research. The emphasis at UCSC was to be on high-quality liberal arts and science programs for the purpose of educating the whole person, rather than narrowly trained technocrats and bureaucrats (McHenry, 306). Over time, however, the school began to copy the methods of the universities it was designed to distinguish itself from, and slowly developed into a research organization. In the beginning it advertised itself as a university primarily dedicated to undergraduate teaching and continued to do so long after the emphasis had shifted to graduate and research programs. Only recently has it begun to admit this change has occurred. It now advertises itself as a research university with strong graduate and undergraduate programs.

Today, UCSC takes in over $100 million annually in grants, contracts and gifts for research in engineering, biomolecular science, ocean sciences, astronomy and other fields. It administers the Lick and Keck Observatories and Long Marine Lab, and in 2003 ranked first in the nation for academic research impact in the field of space sciences. It is also highly rated in the fields of physics and physical sciences, and manages a $330 million NASA Ames contract for space mission research.

UCSC is proud of its research accomplishments, which is warranted because many or even all of these ventures are of high quality. But there is confusion between this research emphasis and the education of most students. Universities build their reputations on research yet try to attract students and funding as educational institutions. Students, parents and taxpayers who notice this will realize that support for these schools is misplaced if one thinks that students, particularly undergraduates, are going to be well educated in an atmosphere dominated by other concerns. There are always exceptions, of course. Some useful training courses are offered, and dedicated teachers and students still exist, but they are no longer of primary interest to research universities and to schools that follow their lead.

If citizens are going to support these institutions, they have a right to insist that educational priorities be made transparent. If universities want to become research institutions, they should do so, but without confusing this with a supposed high-level teaching mission. They currently enjoy non-profit status and have government financial support as teaching institutions, but we may wonder why their profit-making enterprises should not be treated as private business ventures. It is difficult to see the educational benefit of licensed research to most students, or the cost benefit to the public, who pay to underwrite the research with tax dollars, and then buy the products developed at retail prices.

Universities today no longer enjoy wide-scale public support and the largess of surplus government budgets and are trying to find new ways to grow and supplement income. Students still flock to prestigious schools, but in time people may wonder why they should support or attend schools that have more interest in specialized commercial research and certain socio-political positions than in teaching basic learning skills.

Undergraduate education has been suffering disintegration for a long time due to ideological academic battles and confusions in the curriculum, and more recently from the emphasis on specialized research over teaching. Consider this: while we heap abuse on the primary and secondary schools for their failures to educate students, we rarely blame the institutions that educate the educators. This is a problem that involves more than the education departments; it encompasses all of higher education. Despite the billions of dollars spent on education in this country, large numbers of students are poorly prepared. We blame the elementary and high schools for this but continue to believe that many of our universities are "world class" educational institutions. But it is highly doubtful that our Founders would consider them "world class" if they fail to address the educational needs of most students.

University mission statements traditionally list teaching as the first priority, but if one looks at what many universities actually do, another priority comes into view. Few if any identify themselves as superior because of teaching excellence; rather, it is because of research, and much of this research and writing involves very few students. The University of California, for example, celebrates having 50 or so Nobel Prize winners among its schools, and promotes this as an indication of its status as a high-quality teaching institution.

Two things about this publicity need analysis. For one thing, universities double-count prize winners. There are reports showing one winner being listed by two or three different universities because of some sort of part-time presence at each one (Krieger, B4). More disturbing than this dubious scoring system is the fact that it is used for promotional purposes to attract students and donations. The impression given is that these researchers have regular contact with students and influence the learning experience of many. A few of these scholars may teach a sizable number of students, but they are not hired primarily for that. We may be sure that research and prestige take precedence, and for most, the nature of their Nobel quality research leaves little time for undergraduate teaching, or any teaching, apart from working with a few graduate students.

The real issue is not a question of research OR teaching. In-depth research is essential not only for specialized projects but for all good teaching. But increasingly, the professor is becoming a researcher for special projects rather than a researcher for instructional purposes. This is an important reason that we are experiencing a major breakdown in undergraduate education. Some useful training courses are offered, but with little interest in teaching, universities attract and treat students as consumers, providing plush accommodations and an array of courses that may interest and entertain them, but may provide little substantive learning. The result is the current disordered and fragmented curriculum, which offers students a smorgasbord of courses with little correlation between them and with little or no sense of general purpose.

We excuse this state of affairs by saying that the explosion of knowledge in our time makes integration impossible. But if that is true, how do we sustain a community or a nation? Early Americans were of a mind that a cohesive social structure could not be maintained without a more or less common understanding of acceptable individual and communal goals. Historically, education has been given the task of dealing with this problem. Students were to learn useful skills, but in the context of family, community and national values. In our day, we should seriously consider the fact that the failure to tackle this fundamental purpose of education originates in the universities – not in elementary and secondary schools – and it is a failure that has serious ramifications. Because there is no core or foundation for the curriculum, students are exposed to pieces of this or that field of study without an overall view of how these packets of information fit together. It explains why many teachers are poorly prepared and why it is not unusual for students to come away from this experience with little more than the conviction that things are not right in the world.

In 1990, Page Smith, the founding Provost of UCSC, was dismayed to see his original liberal arts vision of the school being disassembled. He had long disapproved of the emphasis on publishing over teaching in universities, although he was widely published himself. UCSC was supposed to be different, but it had moved in the same research/publishing direction. The curriculum was losing focus, growing helter-skelter toward questionable alternatives in an unbalanced way. He estimated that about one-fifth of the total humanities-social science faculty members were avowed Marxists, advocating radical and potentially dangerous changes in American economic and social practices. But even so, Smith thought that the damage would be minimal due to their ineffectual and confusing teachings.

Regarding women's studies, while he had supported women's education for years, he found it impossible to justify the 80 or so courses he counted in feminism. Most were taught by radical feminists with no sense of objectivity or interest in thoughtful investigation. He wondered how young women students could possibly benefit from such a distorted picture of reality. "The image that women carry away with them on graduation must be of a world hopelessly divided into exploiting males and oppressed females. It is one thing to say that women should have their proper place in all disciplines and departments of a university and another to turn over the enterprise to the most militant of their sex" (Smith, *Killing the Spirit*, 291).

Programs like these foster dissension and negativity, with no unifying or productive goal except to upend capitalists, republicans (small "r"), males and the family. They crowd out other areas of knowledge and restrict rather than broaden education. The trend at UCSC and many other schools has continued. Today, the number of non-core and current events courses at UCSC is astounding. There are courses in fashion, movies, TV, hip-hop, and almost countless courses in ethnic and race studies, class struggle, Marxism, gender, sexism, sexual preferences and just plain sex. There are courses in social activism for one cause or another, and recently a conference was held to teach students how to protest. USCS's original idea of a university (*uni-versus* – to turn toward one truth) had become a center for diversity (*di-versus* – to turn in many directions).

UCSC is by no means alone in this trend. But because the liberal studies and undergraduate emphasis of UCSC was so clearly spelled out in the beginning, it offers a stark example of how higher education has changed in this country. As already mentioned, not all colleges and universities are part of this trend. But schools that still try to do undergraduate education well must struggle to avoid becoming part of it. The core curriculum of earlier days is becoming rare.

University Moral Standards

Another concern is the moral atmosphere of college life. A university education today typically has little room for moral discipline. This would be a major concern for the Founders, who believed that self-control was a basic characteristic of free people. One area that seems almost out of control in some schools is sex on campus. Schools now provide abundant resources for sex education and birth control. Yale hands out about 40,000 condoms each year to students, and on Valentine's Day gives away safe-sex kits including condoms, lubricants and directions on how to use them. Also tucked in is information on abstinence, which must seem out of place and confusing to students. Each year incoming freshmen are invited to safer-sex workshops to educate these youngsters, not on self-restraint but on the risks of unprotected sex. Then there is Sex Week, which brings in experts, including prostitutes and sex-shop personnel, to do demonstrations with sex toys and techniques.

Yale may be more aggressive in promoting sex than some other universities, but it is an example of what others also are doing. Male and female students live in the same dormitories, and even in the same suites, and birth control devices with detailed instructions are given to students. The University of Chicago has Educational Guidelines that teach students "good practices" when engaging in sexual activity. UC Berkeley does likewise, although it had to suspend one sex course, offered for credit, after students and their instructor were involved in an orgy and discovered "studying" at a San Francisco sex club. Schools think they are protecting students by assuming they are having sex and teaching them how to do it. Lip service may be given to abstinence, but the overall atmosphere in higher education is infected by a culture of sexual "freedom" (Harden, Sex *and God at Yale* and *The College Fix*; Trounson and Silverstein; University of Chicago).

There is increasing evidence that these supposedly avant-garde university policies are doing real harm. The American College of Pediatricians "strongly endorses abstinence-until-marriage sex education and recommends adoption by all school systems in lieu of 'comprehensive sex education'," which is what schools call their sex programs. The pediatricians want abstinence education because of what they see happening to young people who are sexually active. Pelvic diseases, infertility, herpes, HIV and other diseases are affecting large numbers of young people. Based on their own experiences and information from many other sources, these doctors find that sexually transmitted diseases are widespread in the U.S. Half of the 19 million cases reported annually occur in teens and young adults. In addition to physical diseases are the many problems associated with abortion, or, if not that, of pregnancy, child-raising and increased risks of poverty. There are multiple incidents of depression connected with these issues for both girls and boys.

"Comprehensive sex education" is not a viable answer to these problems. Schools mishandle information and tacitly encourage sex among youth. Studies show that the frontal cortex of the adolescent brain is not fully developed and is unable to make consistently sound judgments, which makes young people overly susceptible to the influences of sexually charged atmospheres.

> Consequently, when it comes to sex education, adolescents need to be given clear direction repeatedly, as is done with programs that address smoking, drugs and alcohol use.
>
> Emphasis on contraceptive methods undermines the authority of parents and the strength of the abstinence message....
>
> Adolescents need repetitive, clear and consistent guidance. (American College of Pediatricians)

The universities may think they are somehow advancing knowledge with their sex education, but many doctors and parents are discovering that attempts by schools to accommodate and even promote sex while preaching against diseases, pregnancy and harassment is a confusing and destructive combination.

In this new age of "liberation," one would think there ought to be at least some room left for the virtue of self-restraint. It is a necessary dimension of human freedom but that subject is not on the agenda of today's sex education, except in passing. But it is important, not only because of what these doctors say but also because it is a significant factor in self-esteem. Educators worry about student self-esteem and depression, but often do not connect that with self-control, which enhances feelings of self-worth. A great deal more attention to this relationship is needed.

Adding to the confusion of young students trying to grow up is the aggressive prosecution of sexual harassment claims. On the one hand, sex is accepted on campus and even encouraged, but on the other anyone accused of inappropriate sexual activity is severely punished. In some cases the accusation alone is sufficient to pronounce a guilty verdict. Hearings or trials on campus have been known to prevent the accused from offering a defense or even attending the hearing. The rules of the proceedings typically are not based on the presumption of innocence but on the preponderance (51 percent) of guilt or innocence, determined by the "evidence" provided only by the accuser (Bader). This is far removed from our historical principles protecting the rights of the accused.

The best known example of this kind may be the Duke University-Lacrosse Team fiasco of 2006. In this case, a stripper claimed that she had been raped by Duke lacrosse players. The immediate reaction of the University was to condemn the accused, cancel the lacrosse schedule and fire the coach. The only evidence of guilt was the accusation of the stripper. Players were arrested and charged and the county District Attorney claimed he was certain they were guilty. Only after these players sued and spent a great deal of money and time defending themselves did the D.A. relent. Duke finally had to admit that the charges were false. The woman was never prosecuted, although she had been arrested on other charges before this episode and was later jailed for stabbing her boyfriend to death ("Durham-In-Wonderland").

Another sign of moral confusion on campus is a call by over 100 college presidents to seriously consider lowering the drinking age (College Presidents). This, they think, will alleviate the widespread problem of student binge drinking. But any proposal that tries to curtail excessive drinking of youngsters by making it easier to drink is bound to be met with skepticism or even ridicule. Still, there is a more important reason to question this approach. Regardless of what the optimum drinking age might be, we need to ask what the schools themselves are doing about this situation. Do they admit any responsibility for dealing with it, or are they simply saying that it is not their problem and we must look to elected officials, judges and policemen for the answer?

Some of these presidents may be truly interested in their students' welfare, and all probably think they are showing genuine concern by publicly highlighting a hazardous issue, but in doing so they avoid accountability themselves. This glaring omission might escape them however, due to the culture of non-involvement that pervades much of contemporary education. Student conduct often is not a major concern, especially off-campus, and because of this student life can become an almost unrestrained free-for-all.

One reason schools shy away from enforcing standards of behavior is the intense competition for students and tuition income. Financial concerns create a strong temptation to relax discipline and increase creature comforts for students in order to present a welcoming, accepting atmosphere. As might be expected, along with this comes a reluctance to provide the adult supervision that is needed, especially for younger students.

Instead of calling for a national discussion of drinking laws, it might be better to call for a review of the teaching mission of higher education. There could be in-depth discussions on teaching as a priority, the responsibility of faculty and administrators to set a high moral tone, the establishment of clear policies on drinking and other behavioral matters and definite rules for enforcement of policies. A strong case could be made for a no tolerance policy on binge drinking, drug use and other unacceptable behaviors both on and off campus.

Rather than abdicating responsibility and turning to the law for a remedy, educators should be in the vanguard, teaching and promoting the principles and behaviors of civilized people. The forgotten principle *in loco parentis* requires academic accountability for student well-being. In our day such thinking is often regarded as a quaint leftover from the past, supposedly having no place in the world of emancipated students and avant-garde intellectual pursuits. But the problem is that many young people are not yet mature enough to be left on their own. By ignoring this obvious fact, higher education fails to guide students by helping them integrate new knowledge into a healthy and productive lifestyle.

Dependency and the Life of Comfort

Demanding course work will keep some students occupied, but at the other educational extreme is a laissez-faire, indirect approach that demands little, relies on shallow treatment of course content and inculcates an attitude of passive entitlement. This attitude would be anathema to the Founders because it removes personal responsibility. Concern for student "adjustment," "happiness" and "self-esteem" take precedence over academic competence. The philosophy behind this seems to be based on a belief that students can learn in their own way, without much discipline or hard work.

Apart from any philosophical or psychological explanations for this attitude, the financial considerations mentioned above are reasons to offer undemanding courses. Enrollments increase and tuition income grows as colleges and universities attract students with plush physical comforts on campus while tolerating minimal achievement in order to keep them in school. The problem is that this approach neither promotes substantive learning nor does it help develop strong character traits.

Also to be noticed is the effect of an undemanding atmosphere on a young person's attitude toward life in general. Studies are now appearing showing that young adults accustomed to the joys of an unrestrained childhood have special difficulties adjusting to the realities of the adult world. Without the support of indulgent parents and teachers, earlier satisfaction may be replaced by sadness, listlessness and depression. Accustomed to comfort, praise and "understanding" regardless of what they do, the experience of failure does such students in. Those who have been pampered and never challenged at home do not adjust well to more demanding circumstances. Once faced with actual restrictions, although few remain in contemporary education, and with D's and F's instead of stickers saying "Good Try," or trophies for finishing last, they lose hope.

Depression among students is a growing problem. Imagine, for example, the frustration of a pampered freshman being introduced to the bewildering atmosphere of a large university campus. The myriad of courses offered, the disconnected content of many of them, the lack of adult guidance or supervision, the struggle for grades and the uninhibited social scene could cause even the most stable student to waver. Four or more years of a young person's life in these circumstances can take an unhealthy toll.

Once in the workforce, students who have been raised in soft or disorienting environments have difficulty adjusting. Lacking the experience of hardship, or, after enduring years of college stress and unproductivity, it could be difficult for them to work effectively as part of a business community. Most of these students probably overcome such impediments eventually, but until then they will not able to think much beyond their immediate needs. They are more likely to ask, "What can this company do for me?" than "What can I do for this company?"

There is a note of cynicism in this outlook, based on frustration over the failure of institutions and authorities to provide everything wished for. It can create angry resentment and protests directed at family members, businesses, politicians and government officials. This is not protesting in order to improve conditions for everyone; it is protest solely for self-interest. It contributes to the feeling that each person is alone in this life and must make the best of it however one can, regardless of the consequences. That could account for protesters demanding things that benefit only themselves, and for the glaring inconsistency of hating and reviling business and government while at the same time accepting welfare, donations and grants. It is like the double-standard found among children who reject their parents, but not their money.

The Cult of Self

> *A talkative writer cornered an unsuspecting victim at a cocktail party. He dominated the conversation talking on and on about himself until he finally stopped to say," Enough about me. Let's talk about you. How did you like my latest book? "*

Self-interest is a natural condition, but excessive self-interest in a democratic republic can be especially corrosive because of the free rein citizens enjoy. People are allowed to pursue their passions more than is possible in dictatorial states, and while this can lead to unusually creative outcomes, it can also promote unsocial and damaging forms of individualism. Prime examples of this are Wall Street executives, company CEOs and school/university administrators who take salary increases and huge bonuses while their companies, clients and students struggle financially. There are egregious examples of members of Congress legislating programs that provide lavish retirement and health benefits for themselves, but not for other citizens.

These kinds of actions are often clandestine and quietly implemented, but other more in-your-face selfish behaviors can be found among black and white racists, strident feminists, student activists, union organizers and others who try to intimidate their oppressors, real or imaginary. Even granting the legitimacy of some of these causes, the way they are advocated raises questions regarding their connection to authentic constitutional freedom.

The recent happenings in Madison, Wisconsin illustrate this. Wisconsin's serious debt situation made it clear that State-wide belt-tightening was critically needed and that this included trimming the benefit packages of public union members. Current and future payments could not be sustained without large, unaffordable tax increases. Governor Scott Walker's budget proposal dealt with this by limiting union collective bargaining and by requiring member contributions to pensions and benefits. This brought out huge protests. As many as 70,000 union members and others from Wisconsin and around the country overwhelmed downtown Madison, shouting and demanding their "rights" and "freedoms." Many were University of Wisconsin professors, students and local teachers. Holding up "Freedom" signs and waving American flags, they agitated for union benefits. The Capitol was occupied. The Governor and his family were threatened. Intimidation of this sort went on day and night for weeks.

The situation became so heated that protesting teachers, fearing loss of pay for missing school, were encouraged to keep demonstrating by University physicians who set up tables on site and wrote sick excuses for anyone who asked. Some lawmakers fled to Illinois to prevent a quorum from forming to pass the budget (Kelleher and Bailey; ABC News). Regardless of the merits of the case, these tactics call into question how freedom and the rule of law are understood by these protestors. Their efforts were closer to mob action than democratic debate.

Despite all the harassment, the budget finally did pass and new rules for union bargaining and contributions became law. But this did not end the protests. A huge effort to recall the Governor followed, but failed. He won by a bigger margin of victory in the recall than in the prior election. Still, protests continue. The unions have now found a federal judge willing to invalidate the new law. This, of course, will be appealed by Wisconsin to a higher court, and the fight will go on as union members there and elsewhere continue to demand what they believe are their "rights," regardless of the impact on the rest of the community.

Language and National Identity

Schools teach a variety of foreign languages, which are of value because they broaden student awareness and enrich the educational experience. But great emphasis is now being placed on the rights of immigrants to have their own languages officially accepted publicly. This is promoted by some educators but also by immigrant or nationalist groups trying to enhance the nation's commitment to tolerance, equality and freedom. The problem is that it interferes with another American commitment: the obligation to foster national unity. Our Founders struggled mightily with this issue. Aside from all the political disagreements they faced, they saw how important it was to improve communication between and within the states by using a single national language. We can be certain that Noah Webster would be appalled today by public signs, statements and directions being written in foreign languages. He would be even more disturbed by non-English election ballots. Much of his life's work was devoted to fostering national unity by promoting an American form of English that could be used by all citizens. He knew that the widespread use of several native languages would defeat that goal, and with it the sense of togetherness vital to the democratic republic.

One can imagine Webster's reaction to recent demonstrations over immigration laws combined with celebrations of separate national identities and languages. He, of course, was part of a long history of accepting foreigners into this country. That was not the problem. The problem he foresaw was that national groups would turn inward and not wish to assimilate into American culture. Until recently this has been a relatively short-term issue with most ethnic groups. Although there have been difficulties, immigrants have put their native ways aside publicly and been able to incorporate themselves into their new nation. But now, justified by the so-called ethics of "diversity" and "tolerance," we are expected to acknowledge native origins and cultures in themselves, without reference to American citizenship. All of our Founders would surely object to any movement or practice that promoted national or group characteristics at the expense of American oneness.

Their faith was expressed by "E Pluribus Unum." This principle does not disrespect individual family backgrounds, nationalities, races, religions or customs, but it does not approve of defiant public displays and government programs that may be well-meaning but actually create tensions and misunderstandings. Americans have always been expected to subordinate their foreign allegiances to those of their new home. America is a melting pot, and its success depends on citizens appreciating this country more than the one they came from.

EPILOGUE

Why American Democracy Requires a Fundamental Reform of Education

S chools are now involved in issues of politics, sex, discrimination, the environment and other current interests, but most discussions on educational reform still center on improvements in job training, and most of that is connected with calls for more funding and better technological instruction. But the huge increases in spending of recent years and the new emphasis on math and science have not improved student achievement much, if at all. Given that we already pay astronomical amounts for education and now stress science and technology, it should occur to us that there may be a deeper problem in education than lack of money or technical training.

How Old Ideas Help Make the Curriculum New Again

Perhaps it would help to reconsider the goals of education from an historical perspective. It probably would surprise most of the population today to learn that job preparation was not the only goal of education for early Americans, nor was it the primary goal. Training of that kind was necessary, but, as Noah Webster and many others said, more important, especially in early life, was preparation for living in a free, democratic society. Learning involved more than job preparation; the successful student also had to understand the citizen's role in society. In that light, it is easy to see why so much emphasis was placed on moral education. As we saw, Webster's books were full of moral lessons, as were the writings and speeches of many of his contemporaries.

It is worth repeating Webster's assessment: every locality should have a school taught by the most reputable and well-informed person in the district. The usual branches of learning should be taught, as well as the principles of virtue. "The virtues of men are of more consequence to society than their abilities, and for this reason, the heart should be cultivated with more assiduity than the head." This was not the assessment of an anti-intellectual; Webster was one of the leading scholars of his time.

As we have seen, he was not alone in this conviction. Exhortations to moral competence were commonplace:

Benjamin Franklin – education should encourage service to "Mankind, one's Country, Friends and Family… and should indeed be the great Aim and End of all Learning."

John Adams (to his son, John Quincy) – "You will ever remember that all the end of study is to make you a good man and a useful citizen. This will ever be the sum total of the advice of your affectionate father."

Benjamin Rush – after the war, the Revolution continues, he said, as attention is given to "the principles, morals and manners of our citizens for these new forms of government…"

George Washington – "every valuable end of Government is best answered by the enlightened confidence of the people; and by teaching the people themselves to know and to value their own rights…"

Later, Ralph Waldo Emerson captured that outlook – "The great object of Education should be commensurate with the object of life. It should be a moral one…"

Education of this kind is a critical necessity for a democracy; it points the way from isolated self-interest to communal interest and the realization that freedom depends upon a shared regard for the common good.

It was clear to our Founders that citizens had to know moral principles and seriously try to practice them for the sake of family, occupation, society and the democratic way of life. The term "virtue" was not a watered-down notion of "kindness" or "goodness," but the classical idea of courage, integrity, respect, fidelity, honesty, strength and self-restraint – the characteristics of honorable and useful citizens. The Founders were aware that people through the ages had always hoped that their kings, dictators or ruling elite would be virtuous, but now in the New World came the realization that the people themselves were the rulers and the need for virtue fell directly upon them.

The contrast between this idea of freedom and current notions is striking. Today, the moral dimension has diminished as a priority in public schools and is actually forbidden if teachings are even slightly connected with religion. Some private and sectarian schools may give traditional ideas and practices more attention, but it cannot be assumed that they do. The pressure to conform to current trends is great. Yale, as we saw, blatantly upends traditional beliefs on sexual morality and self-control, as do other schools (See *University Moral Standards* on pages 163-167). The causes for this situation are many, but the result is clear: moral education, as understood by our Founders, is no longer a meaningful goal of education in this country.

The abandonment of this early American idea of education is surely a primary reason that contemporary education so often fails to inspire learning and the desire for competence. Additional funding and specialized training will not correct this deficiency. We need to recognize that it is possible and desirable to introduce traditional moral principles into American education without fear of proselytizing in public schools. The disciplinary aspect can be reinstituted without any reference to religion, and if the classroom approach is historical, moral principles can be taught without advocating any specific church doctrine. To say that they are Christian is an historical fact; one need not join a church or even be a Christian to acknowledge that. The entire educational experience could be much improved by incorporating this neglected but basic dimension of western education. It should not be difficult to show that moral or character education promotes the desire for learning and proficiency and requires the discipline necessary to achieve success. The benefit for society and the nation is self-evident.

Our schools must do better, but we should acknowledge the difficulty of their task. Family atmosphere, the media, movies, TV and other cultural influences play major roles in education, much of it harmful. The family is the primary educator, and without parental involvement it is difficult for educators to be successful. Apathy in the home undermines student academic performance, but on the other hand, too much family input can become obstructive. It may be caused more by a frantic effort to get family members into the "right" colleges than to improve education for all. Parents who hover over their children constantly and badger teachers about their grades do not help matters. Children need guidance but also a certain amount of freedom to learn from their own experiences.

If political interests in education today were to correspond with those of our Founders, American education no doubt would look much different and be much better than it is. Private schools have their own problems with quality education, but public schools have the added burden of dealing directly with politicians and government officials who have assumed unhealthy jurisdictional control. Intelligent family involvement and local control are critical ingredients for improved education. In the absence of that, we can look forward to increased government interference and poorer results, regardless of how much money is spent or how the system is organized.

Character Education and Religion

There probably would be much more moral education in the schools were it not for the threat of lawsuits over religion. The thought of litigation costs petrifies administrators whenever advocates of secularism threaten to sue over church-state issues. The major casualty in this is that moral education gets swept out the door along with religion. The problem is not that proselytizing of specific church beliefs is forbidden, which it should be in public schools, but that underlying western moral principles that have religious and philosophical roots are eliminated from the curriculum and disciplinary structure of the school.

"Discipline" has almost become a taboo word, but it need not be understood as brute force and angry punishment. Although it has often been associated with punishment, that is not its real meaning. Traditionally, it has meant instruction and guidance. It is the attentive direction that teachers extend to disciples, i.e., students. It is related to such words as "decent," "doctor," "dignity" and "decorous." It is the kind of training that develops the mental faculties and integrates intellectual learning with behavior. Initially, discipline is received from external sources (parents, teachers), but gradually is internalized to the point where the student becomes self-directed. It is the foundation of learning, requiring personal organization, direction and purpose. In the Bible it is called "wisdom" (Wisdom 1:5, 7:14; Sirach 6:18, 23), the attribute of the true teacher and the goal of the true student. Discipline teaches respect for persons and ideas, and provides the orientation necessary for productive personal growth and the sense of self-worth.

Disciplinary practices promote awareness of personal strengths and weaknesses, and the corresponding meaning of human dignity and potential. They also provide the setting for appreciation of age-old religious and philosophical teachings on moral character. They are the framework used by our forebears for teaching the virtues of faith, hope, love, justice, prudence, temperance and courage. They also encourage us to face human imperfections, called "sins" in the Bible, and to take responsibility for personal faults instead of pointing the accusing finger elsewhere.

Another lost dimension of learning, closely related to discipline, is physical activity. One can only learn so much sitting behind a desk. Varsity sports are still considered part of school life, but intramural sports and physical education on all levels have fallen behind. This is most apparent in universities where varsity programs dominate almost everything, including academics, but it also applies to elementary and secondary schools. Physical activities for all students on all levels deserve a higher priority. They are important for health reasons and the development of physical strength and dexterity, and also for the lessons games can teach about competition and cooperation.

One part of physical learning that essentially has been lost altogether is manual work at school. Once expected of students, it is no longer thought important, and because of that, valuable learning experiences are missed. Benjamin Franklin understood this. He built into his curriculum agricultural and mechanical work for the students. The most obvious place where this type of learning is applied today is in gardening and manual arts programs. These are helpful, but a broader approach would engage all students in simple tasks that contribute to the physical learning environment. They usually have chores to do at home; they could also have chores at school. Even light physical tasks can teach skills that help students learn the values of organization and cooperation. If such tasks also make them more aware of the effort required to maintain a classroom and school building, their efforts could instill a sense of pride in the school. Students should not be considered passive consumers. If they play active parts in the overall operation of the school, even on the most basic level, they can begin to see themselves as participants and contributors rather than just recipients of education.

To improve education its overall purpose must be addressed. General education, the province of K-12 and undergraduate education, has never been designed to produce specialists – until now. The idea in our country has been to develop competent citizens, capable of learning and contributing to any number of enterprises as adults. This cannot be done by demanding more time for math, for example, at the expense of history. A more general, but more demanding curriculum is needed in all areas. Specialization can come later, after students are grounded in basic areas of knowledge. Specialists who come forth from a broadly based education have the advantage of being able to adapt to changing circumstances and to apply new knowledge constructively. As we saw, some business leaders are now making this argument (White; Augustine; Berkowitz. See page 150).

The current all-out campaign to advance math and science programs in schools is leaving other studies behind and so far has shown little progress overall. School testing results give almost no indication of improved outcomes for most students. One reason for this is that math and science by themselves do not satisfy the need for total educational development. Unless they are integrated well with other parts of the curriculum the results will be mixed at best. Some technically oriented students may benefit, but even they will suffer from lack of exposure to other areas of knowledge.

Religion and History in a New Curriculum

Consider a school designed to develop good and useful citizens – the kind that John Adams wanted for his son. Each day would include time for silent meditation and prayer, and time for Bible reading and instruction. As outlandish as that may sound today, it has been the rule rather than the exception through most of our history. The Bible is a seminal influence in the development of western civilization and should be part of every student's education, regardless of personal religious beliefs. If we are ever able to come to our senses regarding the inaccurate and misapplied principle of church-state separation, prayer and Bible study probably would reappear in most schools. At least such things would not be banned, as they are today. In keeping with customs established by Jefferson and Madison, students who object to this would not be obliged to participate, but they would not be able to deny others the right to engage in these traditional practices. Ideally, the form and method of these activities would be determined by each local school district and college.

Another overlooked area is history. Instead of using history courses to promote current social and political ideologies, as is often done, emphasis could be placed on substantive courses in world history, and especially in European and American history. Entire courses could be devoted to the Declaration of Independence, the Constitution and the writings of the Founders. Among other things, these studies would inform students of the American meaning of freedom and its connection with property rights and general education.

These ideas and practices are integral parts of the American heritage. They have religious underpinnings, but public schools need not be put off by that. They can be justified as historically successful methods of teaching that influenced our Founders and the form of government they created. It is not necessary to be a church-goer to appreciate these principles, but their historical context must be respected if they are to be understood correctly. Constitutional government is built on these concepts, and citizens need to value them if democracy is to have any chance of functioning as it should. As such they belong in American education because they help students, whatever their religious views, understand what our democracy is and how it functions. At the same time, students can gain appreciation for their own strengths, weaknesses, rights and responsibilities as human beings and members of society. The application of these insights to skills training and job preparation is self-evident.

Western moral values are still alive in this country, but they are being weakened by an educational system that either implicitly or formally ignores them. It is a testament to the character of young people today that so many are respectful of others and concerned about the poor, the environment and other social matters. But we cannot assume these good traits will endure in the future if the nation continues to move away from its moral heritage. Attempts are made in public schools to teach ethics, but they are limited to philosophical and psychological approaches that do not bring out the fundamentals of our moral tradition. They have value, as do studies of the moral teachings of other religions, but they are incomplete because our own religious teachings are purposely excluded due to misinterpretations of First Amendment church-state separation.

Good teachers and professors teach moral values mainly by example. Teaching by example is important, to be sure, but students should also be formally exposed to the historical religious teachings that have influenced the American people. This can be done without proselytizing or advocating any specific form of Christianity or Judaism. The moral dimension in particular should become an explicit part of the entire curriculum in both public and private schools.

Human behavior is determined to a large extent by how people think, and what they think about. If they are taught to hate, as the Nazis were, and today's terrorists are, their ideas can cause incredible destruction. But if they are taught to value integrity, personal responsibility, productivity and respect for their country, much good can come of that. Americans believe in these things, but our current educational culture de-emphasizes them. Instead, it focuses on individualistic self-interest, victimhood and denial of western values under such headings as "diversity" and "tolerance." Efforts along these lines are intended to create "a level playing field," "equality" and "fairness," but they can weaken rather than strengthen the sense of personal dignity and capability.

People truly in need must be helped, but not necessarily by government, and not by programs that foster a cult of helplessness. People who can be convinced that they are being oppressed and cannot better themselves will naturally seek a scapegoat to blame and turn to others for help. What follows are political solutions that are supposed to aid those in need but more often have the effect of taking power away from the people and giving it to government regulators, lawyers and judges. This not only opens the door to excessive government interference, but makes it more difficult for youth to grasp the meaning of citizenship in a nation that was originally built on principles of self-reliance and political freedom.

According to Friedrich Hayek, who witnessed the rise of Nazism in Germany, the movement began as an effort by socialists of good will to improve economic and social conditions. He watched as they worked to implement their programs by gradually increasing the role of government as provider of benefits. This led to government control over the means of production and distribution. Eventually the well-intentioned socialist goal was transformed into a fascist movement dominated by power-hungry government authorities. Many of the original socialists abandoned the movement for moral reasons but by that time their government had become totalitarian.

Hayek spent his early years in Austria where he saw this transformation take place in Germany. In his later years he lived in the United States and was alarmed to see the same kind of transition taking place. America was on the path to socialism, he said, which inevitably leads to autocratic government control. The reason is that socialist planning tries to create economic equality, not by encouraging the less fortunate to become more productive but by taking from the rich to give to the poor. Ultimately this can only be done by force. If one imagines that an employee's freedom is restricted by a wealthy and demanding employer, he said, that pales in comparison to the power of one bureaucrat backed by an authoritarian government. He saw how bureaucrats in Germany controlled not only economic activity but almost all aspects of life (Hayek, *passim*). His experience taught that having good intentions is not enough. Good-willed beginnings can end with almost the opposite of what was originally intended.

Does Voting Matter?

> A democracy is always temporary in nature...[It] will continue to exist up until the time voters discover that they can vote themselves generous gifts from the public treasury. From that moment on, the majority always votes for the candidates who promise the most benefits from the public treasury, with the result that every democracy will finally collapse over loose fiscal policy [which is] always followed by a dictatorship....The average age of the world's greatest civilizations from the beginning of history has been about 200 years.

This quotation is attributed to Alexander Tyler, an eighteenth century Scot. Whether he said it or not is debated, but somebody did and it has often been quoted. Perhaps the Russian communist mentioned in the

Prologue had it in mind when he said he could not judge the success of American democracy since it was only 200 years old. We may think of it now in view of clamors for more public benefits in the face of our enormous national debt.

One critical sign of political success or failure is the voting mentality of the people. Do they think of government as a defender of individual rights or as a giant benevolent storehouse of free aid and subsidies? How people vote answers this question. If we are at a place now where significant numbers expect free public benefits and vote accordingly, the constitutional structure of the nation is at risk.

This is the problem John Adams addressed when giving advice on voting rights in Massachusetts (Adams, *Letter to James Sullivan*). The history of Rome showed how destructive the voting franchise can be when extended to those who vote to receive public benefits with no corresponding obligation or cost to themselves. Adams firmly believed that when "fairness" and "equality" mean getting something for nothing, neither fairness nor equality ensue. The result is social unrest rather than peace and tranquility.

This bit of wisdom goes back a long way. St. Paul dealt with this problem in churches where some members concluded that Christian freedom meant doing nothing. But their lazy and carefree ways resulted in them becoming dependent on other church members. Paul's solution was to give nothing to those who refused to work. They had to learn that they did not deserve handouts. It was not charity to provide for people able to fend for themselves. In fact, it was the opposite of charity because giving aid to the able-bodied makes them more dependent on others and creates dissension in the community. Charity, he taught, is intended only for the truly needy (See *Work, Property and Human Dignity* on page 71-72).

This is also the lesson of Jamestown and Plymouth. The initial society in both was based on communal ownership and soon began to deteriorate into feuding factions. Some were continually finding excuses for not working; others objected to providing for non-family members;

most complained about the income expected by the investors living in Europe and not working on the plantation. The situation settled down only after private property rights were established, which gave people incentive to benefit directly from their own work (See *Jamestown* and *Plymouth* on pages 21-27).

These colonial experiments were successful but it cannot be assumed that all policies of self-reliance will be. Once people become accustomed to getting government benefits, it becomes extremely difficult to reduce or take them away. The tendency today seems to be in the other direction, i.e., giving more for doing less. But this can eventually ruin people's self-respect and destabilize the economy. If there is an answer to this problem, other than to install a heavily authoritarian government that reduces benefits and institutes strict social controls, it must be the one the Founders promoted, i.e., general education. So far, American education has been a great benefit to our society, but whether or not it will continue to be is an open question. It certainly will not be beneficial if schools and colleges fail to perform the real tasks of education.

Tax laws, social policies, rigid government bureaucracies and other challenges to private property make it imperative that citizens demand genuinely good education and choose carefully where they and their children go to school. It is also essential that they engage in the voting process. One reason so many people today feel disconnected from government and education must be that they do not understand their role in our democratic republic. Many are politically active only when demonstrating for or against something. Too often they know what they want for themselves, but not what benefits the community. In some elections less than half of the eligible citizens bother to vote. Many reject politics completely. People often say they have washed their hands of the whole system and will not vote because all politicians are crooks. But will not politicians represent the people who support them more than those who remove themselves from the political arena and even show contempt for it? We can assume that elected officials will, by and large, represent those who support them, and that includes more than financial supporters. It includes all who might vote for them.

We are in the midst of a gradual government takeover of citizens' constitutional rights and a return to some form of strong-armed rule. But unless Americans lose the will for independence that has been our trademark, strong reaction to this shift can be expected at some point. World history is filled with violent protests against holders of power, yet except for the Civil War and some smaller incidents, America has been able to avoid large-scale rebellions due to its constitutional form and the moral strength of its people. But among those who have lost faith in the rule of law, there is always the prospect of discontent backed by force. Current incidents of riotous street demonstrations, uses of assault weapons, threats against both conservatives and liberals, and against the government itself signal widespread local and national unrest.

Money rules politics, it is said, but much of it goes into campaigning. Why? Because votes count. As our Founders warned, if voters do not care or can be fooled, or vote only according to narrow self-interests, their votes will go to the wrong people. Webster, Adams, Jefferson, Madison and their friends were keenly aware of this danger. But if the people understand how a republic can and should operate, and how important the electorate is in the process, votes will go to candidates who represent communal interests more than self-serving special interests. Inattention to communal interests by ill-informed citizens can result in loss of property rights, including their own, and it can happen without them realizing it. A well-informed electorate, however, can prevent many a power grab by charlatans, special-interests, politicians, judges and others.

Education: The Alternative to Revolution

> If a nation expects to be ignorant and free in a state of civilization, it expects what never was and never will be. (Jefferson, *Letter to Charles Yancey*)

The contrast between ignorance and freedom was in the minds of the Founders from the beginning. It explains their vital interest in the education of a people destined for self-rule. But could the masses be trusted with this power? Could they make decisions based on common needs, or would they succumb to self-interest only? All leaders agreed that government authority was needed, but how much? In 1787 Thomas Jefferson wrote a letter to James Madison about the relationship between a strong central government and an educated populous. This was an important subject at the time because of the conflict between the Federalists' desire for vigorous, or what they called "energetic," central government and the Republican (Democrat) insistence on rule by the people.

> [The question is] whether peace is best preserved by giving energy [power] to the government or information to the people. This last is the most certain and the most legitimate engine of government. Educate and inform the whole mass of the people. Enable them to see that it is their interest to preserve peace and order, and they will preserve them. And it requires no very high degree of education to convince them of this. They are the only sure reliance for the preservation of our liberty.

This was not an either-or argument but a question of where the balance of power should lie. Jefferson and Hamilton were leading protagonists in this debate (Bowers, 29-30; Chernow, 251-260). The Jeffersonians feared the return of a heavy-handed monarchy; the Hamiltonians feared anarchy (Hamilton, *Federalist, No. 70*). The question of education was a major issue. Both sides advocated public education but knew it was less important in a monarchy or aristocracy than in a democracy. This is because a strong central government decides public policy for the people, whereas a democracy decides for itself. An uninformed majority is a special danger in a democracy because ignorant people making their own rules can become little more than an uncontrolled mob.

Hamilton wanted a strong central government more than Jefferson did, but not one imposed on the people. It could be valid only if the people assented to it, and that meant the masses had to be educated. He was a strong-minded Federalist, but one who separated himself from those who desired monarchical, top-down government run by a ruling class. He believed humans have a natural, God-given right to self-government (*The Farmer Refuted*).

The eventual resolution of this conflict was the Constitution. It provided for a central government with definite, but limited powers and the right of the citizens to elect their own representatives to voice their opinions and make laws. The Federalist-Republican (Democrat) conflict continued, but within the confines of the Constitution. The balance of power in the beginning was in favor of the States and the people over the Federal government, but this arrangement called for nationwide education of the people. Without that, the Founders realized that the system could collapse into a lawless society, succeeded by a despotic government.

It has been said that Jefferson won this battle by preserving a strong voice of the people, and that may be true, but Hamilton's approach never died out. Advocates of a powerful federal government lived on and since the Second World War have become much stronger. With this trend, we see government deciding more and the people deciding less. And as citizens become less educated in a real sense, regardless of the time and money spent on schools, government increases its control of the people. Possibly the most obvious sign of this is the ongoing transfer of property rights from individuals to the governments. We have seen how the Judiciary has encouraged this. Primary examples are increased federal and state controls of education, land use and business activities, and the expansion of burdensome federal-state-local tax policies, not only for the rich but for most taxpayers (See "Contemporary Ideas" on pages 73-81 and 133-141).

Freedom requires respect for personal property rights, and respect for those rights requires meaningful education. Nationally, we are not yet thinking in these terms, but to continue as a free people, property rights must be restored and honored, and for that to happen appropriate general education is needed. This education must not only prepare students for work; it must also teach them to value and contribute to a free society. It will teach students to appreciate the history of this republic and the courage, honesty and patriotism of the best of our forebears.

Not all citizens will understand or accept these lessons. But that has always been the case. In the early days not all agreed on the proper course for America's future. There were numerous views on the nature of government and heated arguments over the direction the nation should take. It was a wonder that a unified nation was created at all. Washington believed that winning the War was a miracle, as did many others, and the same can be said about forming our constitutional government. It was due to the wisdom and character of a relatively small number of men that the United States was established. It is not uncommon in history that a few have managed to set the course for a nation, but in this case the few did not grasp authoritarian power only for themselves. Many were surprised that the nation did not become an aristocracy or monarchy. To a great extent political power was left in the hands of the people even though the risks of disintegration were high.

Consider the odds. There was the enormous problem of breaking free from the great power of England, and then the difficulty of dealing with the independent status of the colonies. The differences in their economies and religions created tensions. Some colonies had sizeable industrial and financial interests, others were mainly agricultural. Some were slave free or leaning that way; others were committed to slavery. Some were mainly Congregationalist or Puritan; others were Anglican or Presbyterian, with a substantial presence of Quakers, Baptists and Catholics in many places. These different economic, social and religious interests typically did not mix well and affected the political climate.

The formation of the American Republic was a monumental achievement. Our Founders deserve high praise for that. But we must also recognize that they vigorously disagreed with one another on issues, and sometimes resorted to less than honorable measures. Their failings should not be hidden because they teach the truth about human weaknesses, but neither should they be dwelled upon, as they often are, to the point where the brighter picture of our past and hope for the future is obscured. The point is that despite the Founders' frailties a remarkable union was achieved.

All citizens should know the history and meaning of American freedom and its connection with property rights and general education. To that end, citizens should insist that the education they pay for actually educates. It must provide useful skills as well as an historical understanding of American fundamental human rights and responsibilities. This is important not only for the sake of personal freedom, but also for the sake of communal economic and political freedom. Useful skills training, founded on quality character education is at the heart of this enterprise.

We live in precarious times, but it seems that has always been the case. Wars, corruption, recessions and rebellions have been ongoing threats since the Revolution, but they have not yet destabilized the nation. People still love their freedoms and have high hope for their country's future. Hope for the nation was a driving force at the time of our founding and has continued to be so, although with less single-minded energy than before. Still, it lives on and, if history is any guide, will not die out. Hope of this kind did not originate in America. It has a long history in our heritage going back to the time of Abraham and his people. Its great archetype is the Hebrews' escape from Egypt and journey to the Promised Land. More than once the Exodus nearly ended in disorganization, rebellion and failure, but the people's hope in their future kept the spirit of freedom alive. It has permeated Hebrew and Christian history ever since. It is alive in America today, but it is being seriously challenged by secularist and bureaucratic forces that deny religious values and diminish individual freedom.

If these forces win over the culture, the nation will not survive as a free republic. Our Founders were well aware of this danger. They knew how uncertain their new national experiment with liberty would continue to be. Information that fosters public awareness and personal moral strength was their answer to ever-present threats to the people's sovereignty. The kind of education they envisioned has been a major factor in sustaining the individual freedoms guaranteed by the government they created. It was their solution to tyranny, and it is ours too. The American republic still exists, and given all the challenges it has endured we may wonder why it has not descended into anarchy, dictatorship or despotism. A big part of the answer is found in the traditions and habits of independence that have been instilled and carried along from generation to generation since colonial days. These ideas and habits are deepseated but must be constantly renewed to ensure that the original spirit of freedom does not die out. Preserving that spirit in word and deed is of vital importance to every American today.

ABOUT THE AUTHOR

Gary J. Quinn was born and raised in Monroe, Wisconsin. He attended the University of Wisconsin (B.B.A. – Economics and Business), Catholic University of America (M.A. – Philosophy of Education) and Aquinas Institute of Philosophy and Theology (Ph.D. – Moral Philosophy and Theology). He taught undergraduate and graduate religious studies courses at Loras College, and moral philosophy and theology at Thomas Aquinas Center, Purdue University, where he was University of Notre Dame Visiting Associate Professor of Theology. As a graduate student he taught math and English courses to elementary and high school students.

Dr. Quinn is the author of *Moral Education in America: Its Future in an Age of Personal Autonomy and Multiculturalism*. He has written articles for academic journals and newspapers and has given many public lectures.

His work is influenced by experience in the Navy, as Chief Engineer and Senior Watch Officer aboard USS Snohomish County, and in business, as owner of a real estate finance and investment service. He is active in community service organizations.

He is married with two sons and a daughter-in law, and lives in Scotts Valley, CA.

REFERENCES

Abbreviations: *FC*   *Founders' Constitution*
                         WSJ   *Wall Street Journal*

ABC News. "Wisconsin Doctors Tell Teachers: Call in Sick to Continue Protests." Feb. 19, 2011. www.abcnews.go.com

Adams, J. *Defence of the Constitutions of Government of the United States.* 1787. Vol.1, Ch. 16, #15. *The Founders' Constitution* (hereafter *FC).* University of Chicago Press. www.press-pubs. uchicago.edu

_____ *Constitution of the Commonwealth of Massachusetts.* 1780. *FC,* Vol.1, Ch. 1, #6.

_____ *Inaugural Address.* 1797. www.inaugural.senate.gov

_____ *Letter to James Sullivan.* 1776. *FC,* Vol. 1, Ch. 13, #10.

American College of Pediatricians. *Abstinence Education,* Oct. 2010. www.acpeds.org

Arnn, L. "Whatever Happened to the Ownership Society?" *Imprimis,* Hillsdale College, Nov. 2005.

Augustine, N. "The Education Our Economy Needs." *Wall Street Journal* (hereafter *WSJ*), Sept. 21, 2011. online.wsj.com/article

AUTM. "U.S. Licensing Activity Survey: FY2010." www.inside-highered.com

Bader, H. "Falsely Accused Teachers and Students Will Be Harmed by New Education Department Policy." *Competitive Enterprise Institute*, May 16, 2011. www.cei.org

Berkowitz, P. "Why Liberal Education Matters." *WSJ*, May 15, 2010.

Bleizeffer, D. "Crossing private property." *Casper Star Tribune*, May 3, 2010. www.trib.com

Bovard, J. "What Job 'Training' Teaches?" *WSJ*, Sept. 13, 2011.

Bowers, C. *Jefferson and Hamilton*. New York: Houghton Mifflin, 1925.

Boyer, P. "Jesus in the Classroom." *New Yorker*, March 21, 2005.

Bradford, W. *The Bradford Journal*. Pilgrim Hall Museum, 2005. www.pilgrimhall.org

_____ *Of Plymouth Plantation. FC*, Vol.1, Ch. 16, #1;

_____ *Mayflower Compact. FC,* Vol. 1, Ch. 17, #1.

Bridgewater Deed. Bridgewater Historical Society. www.plymouthcolony.net

Buckman, R. "More Universities Increasing Support for Campus Start-ups." *WSJ*, Nov. 27, 2006.

Bullock, S. "The Specter of Condemnation." *WSJ*, June 24, 2006.

Burke, L. and Muhlhausen, D. "Head Start Impact Evaluation Report Finally Released." Heritage Foundation, January 10, 2013. www.heritage.org/research

Casper Star-Tribune Editorial Board. "Legislature should expand eminent domain discussion." March 11, 2011. www.trib.com

Chaban, M. "There Goes Manhattanville: Supreme Court Turns Down Columbia Expansion Case." *The Observer*, Dec. 13, 2010. www.observer.com

Chernow, R. *Alexander Hamilton*. New York: Penguin Press. 2004.

Coates, E. (ed.). "No. 39. Educating the People." *T. Jefferson on Politics and Government.* Metairie, La. 1995-2001. www.etext.virginia.edu

College presidents. *Amethyst Initiative.* 2008. www.theamethystinitiative.org

"The Cost of Iraq, Afghanistan and other Global War on Terror Operations Since 9/11." *Congressional Research Reports*, May 30, 2008. www.opencrs.com

Dodd, C. *The Apostolic Preaching and its Development.* New York: Harper & Row, 1964.

D'Souza, D. "Created Equal: How Christianity Shaped the West," *Imprimis,* Hillsdale College, Nov. 2008.

"Durham-In-Wonderland," www.duramwonderland.blogspot.com, March 30, 2009; also www.wikipedia.org/wiki/Duke_lacrosse_case

Durkin, E. "Breeze National removed from Columbia U. Manhattanville campus expansion." *New York Daily News*, May 25, 2012. www.mydailynews.com

Elson, H. *History of the United States of America.* New York: MacMillan Co. 1904. www.usahistory.info

Ford, H. *Chicago Tribune*, May 25, 1916.

Franklin, B. *Proposals Relating to the Education of Youth in Pensilvania.* 1749. www.archives.upenn.edu

_____ *On the price of Corn and Management of the Poor.* 1766. www.founding.com

George, H. (Quoted in Smith. P, *Killing the Spirit*, 248).

"George Washington." *New World Encyclopedia.* www.newworldencyclopedia.org

Gerstner, L. "Lessons from 40 Years of Educational 'Reform'." *WSJ*, Dec. 1, 2008. www.online.wsj.com

Goodrich, C. *Lives of the signers to the Declaration of Independence.* New York: W. Reed & Co., 1824. www.colonialhall.com

_____ *A History of the United States.* (edited) 1857. www.celebrateboston.com

Hamilton, A. *Federalist, No. 70. FC*, Vol.1, Ch. 9, #10.

_____ *The Farmer Refuted. FC,* Vol.1, Ch. 3, #5.

Harden, N. *Sex and God at Yale.* New York: St. Martin's Press, 2012.

_____ "Sex, Yale and the Myth of Value-free Education." Sept. 5, 2012. *The College Fix,* Sept. 5, 2012. www.thecollegefix.com

Hayek, F. *The Road to Serfdom.* Abridged edition printed by The Heritage Foundation. Chicago: University of Chicago Press, 1994.

Herrick, T. "Campuses, Companies Cozy Up." WSJ, July 11, 2007.

IBM Corporation. "Curriculum and Assessment." 2012. www.ibm.com

Institute for Justice. "Kelo v. New London." 2006. www.ij.org

Intel Corp. "Curriculum and Assessment." 2012. www.intel.com

Interpreter's Bible, Vol. 1. Nashville, TN: Abington Press, 1952.

Isaacson, W. *Benjamin Franklin.* New York: Simon & Schuster, 2003.

Jaschik, S. "New book criticizes culture of sex at Yale." *Inside Higher Education,* August 23, 2012. www.insidehighered.com

Jefferson, T. *Notes on the State of Virginia.* 1784. *FC,* Vol.1, Ch. 18, #16.

_____ *Letter to James Madison. 1785. FC,* Vol. 1, Ch. 15, #32.

_____ *Letter to James Madison.* 1787. FC, Vol. 1, Ch.18, #21.

_____ *The Virginia Act For Establishing Religious Freedom.* 1786. www.religiousfreedom.lib.virginia.edu

_____ *Letter of the Danbury Baptists.* Oct.7, 1801. www.members. tripod.com *T. Jefferson's reply.* Jan.1, 1802. www.loc.gov/loc/ lcib/9806

_____ *Letter to Charles Yancey.* 1816. www.etext.virginia.edu/jefferson

Jones, J. *Kitzmiller, et.al. v. Dover Area School District, et.al.* U.S District Court (Pennsylvania). Dec. 20, 2005.

Kelleher, J. and Bailey, D. "Largest Crowds since Vietnam War march in Wisconsin." *Reuters,* February 26, 2011. wwwreuters.com

Kelo v. New London. U.S. Supreme Court. June 23, 2005. www.law. cornell.edu

Krieger, L. Stanford stakes its claim to Nobel winners." *Santa Cruz Sentinel,* Oct. 17, 2012.

Leitch, A. *A Princeton Companion.* Princeton: Princeton University Press. 1978. www.etcweb.princeton.edu

Levin, M. *Men in Black.* Washington, D.C.: Regnery Pub., 2005.

Lewis, B. "The Tyrannies Are Doomed." Interview by B. Weiss. *WSJ*, April 2, 2011. online.wsj.com/article

Locke, J. *Thoughts Concerning Education.* 1693. Edited by R. Grant and N. Tarcov. Indianapolis: Hackett, 1996.

_____ *Conduct of the Understanding.* 1697. Edited by R. Grant and N. Tarcov. Hackett, 1996.

_____ *2nd Treatise of Civil Government.* 1685-88. Edited by C. Sherman. New York: Irvington Pub., 1979.

Madison, J. *Letter to W.T. Barry.* 1822. *FC*, Vol.1, Ch. 18, #35.

_____ *Memorial and Remonstrance Against Religious Assessments.* 1785. www.religiousfreedom.lib.virginia.edu

_____ *Property.* 1792. *FC,* Vol.1, Ch. 16, #23.

McCullough, D. *John Adams.* New York: Touchstone, 2001.

McHenry, D. "UCSC: Its Origins....1958-68." Interviewed by E. Calciano. *UCSC McHenry Library*, Vol. 2, 1974.

Mendenhall, G.E. "Ancient Oriental and Biblical Law." *The Biblical Archaeologist*, XVII, #2, 1952.

Mesfin, B. "Cupertino school becomes flash point for religion debate." *Santa Cruz Sentinel*, January 30, 2005.

Montesquieu, C. *Spirit of Laws.* Book 6. *FC,* Vol.1, Ch. 17, #9.

_____ *Spirit of Laws.* Book 8. www.constitution.org/cm

Moore, J. *Prayer in America.* New York: Doubleday, 2005.

Penn, M. "Flight Lessons." Madison: *On Wisconsin*, Winter 2006.

Peterson, P. "Do We Really Need to Spend More on Schools?" *WSJ*, August 5, 2011.

Petulla, S. "University Gains from Licensing Activities." Dec. 20, 2010. *Inside Higher Education.* www.insidehighered.com

Pilgrims and Puritans: Background. American Studies, University of Virginia. www.xroads.virginia.edu

Puls, M. *Samuel Adams.* New York: PalgraveMacmillan. 2006.

Regalado, A. and Hamilton, D. "How a University's Patents May Limit Stem-cell Research." *WSJ,* July 18, 2006.

Rolland, M. "Oklahoma City district...hip-hop curriculum." Oct. 1, 2010. www.newsok.com

Rush, B. *Of the Mode of Education Proper in a Republic. FC,* V.1, Ch. 18, #30.

_____ *A Defence of the Use of the Bible in Schools* www. biblebelievers.com

Sataline, S. "U.S. Judge Rejects Intelligent Design." *WSJ,* Dec. 21, 2005.

Signers of the Declaration of Independence. www.ushistory.org/ declaration

Smith, P. *John Adams.* Vol.1. New York: Doubleday, 1962.

_____ *Killing the Spirit.* New York: Viking, 1990.

Steiner, B.(ed.) *History of Guilford & Madison, Connecticut.* 1897. Guilford Free Library, 1975.

Stohr, G. "Columbia's Expansion Allowed by U.S. Supreme Court in Eminent Domain Case." Dec. 13, 2010.   www.bloomberg. com

Thwaites, R.G. *Epochs of American History: The Colonies.* New York: Longman, 1902.

Tobin, J. "Community Divided Over Tolerance Posters at S.V. High." Feb. 9, 2005. www.SantaCruzSentinel.com

Trounson, R. and Silverstein, S. "Berkeley Class on Sexuality Suspended After Reports of Orgy." *Los Angeles Times,* February 20, 2002. www.articles.latimes.com

U.S. Dept. of Education. "10 Facts About K-12 Education Funding." June 2005. *ED.gov.* www.ed.gov

_____ "Digest of Education Statistics: 2009." *National Center for Education Statistics,* April 2010. www.nces.ed.gov

_____ "The Condition of Education 2011." May 2011. www.nces. ed.gov

U.S. Supreme Court. *Everson v. Board of Education,* 1947; *Engel v. Vitale,* 1962; *Kelo v. New London,* 2005.

University of Chicago. *"Educational Guidelines for Sexual Consent, 2012."* www.csl.uchicago.edu

Walsh, C. "Activism in Action." *Institute for Justice*, August 2010. www.ij.org

Warren, J. "A Brief Biography of George Washington." www.mountvernon.org

Washburn, J. *University, Inc.* New York: Basic Books, 2005.

Washington, G. *First Annual Address to Congress.* January 8, 1790. www.millercenter.org/scripps

_____ *Eighth Annual Message to Congress.* December 7, 1796. www.gwpapers.virginia.edu

_____ *Farewell Address.* September 19, 1796. *FC*, Vol.1, Ch. 18, #29.

Weaver, R. *Ideas Have Consequences.* Chicago: University of Chicago Press, 1948.

Webster, N. *Effects of Slavery on Morals and Industry.* 1793. Hartford: Hudson and Goodwin, 1793. www.amherst.edu/library/archieves

_____ *Oration on Anniversary of the Declaration of Independence.* 1802. lexrex.com/enlightened/writings/webster

_____ *Grammatical Institute.* Hathi Trust Digital Library. www.hathitrust.org

_____ *On the Education of Youth in America.* 1788. *FC*, Vol.1, Ch. 18, #26.

_____ *On the Divizions of Property.* 1790. *FC*, Vol.1, Ch. 15, #44.

_____ *Leading Principles of the Federal Constitution.* 1787. *FC*, Vol.1, Ch. 16, #17.

_____ "Noah Webster." Amherst College Library Exhibit, 2008-09.

_____ "Noah Webster." *Acton Institute.* www.acton.org/publications

Webster's Third International Dictionary. Springfield, MA: Merriam-Webster, Inc. 1993.

White, E. "Future CEOs May Need to Have Broad Liberal-Arts Foundation." *WSJ*, April 12, 2005.

William of St. Thierry. *The Golden Epistle.* Translated by T. Berkeley. Trappist, Kentucky: Cistercian Publications, 1971.

_____ *Three Treatises on Man.* Edited by B. McGinn. Trappist, Kentucky: Cistercian Publications. 1977.

"Williams v. Vidmar, 2005." Alliance Defense Fund, www. alliancedefensefund.org

Williams, R. *The Bloody Tenent, Of Persecution for Cause of Conscience.* 1644. *FC,* Vol.5, Amend 1, #4.

_____ "Roger Williams." *Today in History, February 5.* Library of Congress. www.lcweb2.loc.gov

Wysocki, B. "Columbia's Pursuit of Patent Riches Angers Companies." *WSJ*, December 21, 2004.

Biblical references are from *The New American Bible.* New York: P.J. Kenedy & Sons, 1970.

0000122231137

Made in the USA
San Bernardino, CA
01 November 2013